Bernardo Cho offers biblical theology at it traces the themes of redemption through accessible way. He proves himself an astu late communicator. A true gift. May his labor inspire our ---- God's magnificent grace.

Carmen Joy Imes, PhD
Associate Professor of Old Testament,
Biola University, California, USA

We live in difficult times, especially for the people of God. Some Christians have unashamedly exchanged their "birthright" as conscious participants in the history of salvation for a political "bowl of stew." Others have come to believe that "orthodoxy" can be reduced to one single theological system no matter how alien it may be to the biblical message. Still others have lived with their heads in the clouds, assuming that Christians should wait for a "heavenly nirvana," with no regard for what happens in the real world. In this troubled context a clear understanding of the big picture of Scripture, the biblical plot of redemption, and its implications for the people of God has become an urgent need. My dear colleague, Bernardo Cho, offers precisely this in the present book. And he does it with brilliance, combining solid biblical theology with a remarkable pastoral perspective.

Estevan F. Kirschner, PhD
Professor of Biblical Languages and Exegesis,
Seminário Teológico Servo de Cristo, Brazil

Bernardo Cho has given us a gift. This beautifully written collection deserves deep reading as he walks us through the narrative of Scripture. This is not a tidy rendition that forces pieces to fit and cleans up the rough edges. Rather, Cho invites us to contemplate the fullness of the scriptural message and its characters, as we come to know who God is, how he has worked, and how it is leading to our full restoration. Anyone who has struggled to make sense of why we need the whole Bible, or wondered their place in the grand drama of salvation, is called to meet with God anew and celebrate his purposes for his people and his creation.

Mariam J. Kovalishyn, PhD
Associate Professor of New Testament,
Regent College, Vancouver, Canada

My family and I love to engage in playful activities together. Assembling a puzzle is an example of such moments. It is always an interpretive challenge to look attentively at each piece and to compare them with the larger picture on the box. Reading the Bible entails a similar exercise and Bernardo Cho helps us to do that. He carefully guides us in connecting the loose parts of our understanding of the gospel, correcting them when necessary, and relating each one of them with the biblical story of salvation. This book is an indispensable resource for anyone who wants to integrate the human vocation and the reality of God's presence in the ongoing plot of redemption.

Ziel Machado, DMin
Vice-Rector and Professor of Pastoral Theology,
Seminário Teológico Servo de Cristo, Brazil

Few things are more essential for individual believers and churches to grow in maturity and effectiveness in mission than clear teaching and growing understanding of the word of God. But even in churches where the Bible is regularly preached, it can be done in a random way. Texts are plucked from here and there, as encouraging promises, or as proof texts for favorite doctrines, or occasionally as whips for moralistic lashing. Christians are left ignorant of what the Bible actually *is* as a whole, namely that it tells the great story of God, all creation, and humanity. The Bible explains the past, points us to the ultimate future and calls us to participate now in that story in our present, and to live accordingly. Bernardo Cho sets a fine example of how pastors could help their people grasp that whole Bible story as the framework for deeper exploration of its parts. I am so encouraged to see this book, for its content, for the concept behind it, and for the model it provides for others to emulate.

Christopher J. H. Wright, PhD
Global Ambassador and Ministry Director,
Langham Partnership

Most Christians assume that the point of life is to "go to heaven," and they imagine that this is the story the Bible tells. The reality is far more exciting: that God, the creator, will come and live with us, transforming creation through the work of Jesus and the power of the Spirit. This book sets out this central biblical message excitingly and accessibly. It could revolutionize our hopes, our prayers, and our action in God's world.

N. T. Wright, DPhil
Professor Emeritus of New Testament, University of St. Andrews, UK
Senior Research Fellow, Wycliffe Hall, University of Oxford, UK

The Plot of Salvation

GLOBAL LIBRARY

The Plot of Salvation

Divine Presence, Human Vocation, and Cosmic Redemption

Bernardo Cho

© 2022 Bernardo Kyu Cho

Published 2022 by Langham Global Library
An imprint of Langham Publishing
www.langhampublishing.org

Langham Publishing and its imprints are a ministry of Langham Partnership

Langham Partnership
PO Box 296, Carlisle, Cumbria, CA3 9WZ, UK
www.langham.org

ISBNs:
978-1-83973-627-8 Print
978-1-83973-678-0 ePub
978-1-83973-679-7 Mobi
978-1-83973-680-3 PDF

This work was originally published in Portuguese by Editora Mundo Cristão under the title *O Enredo da Salvação*

Bernardo Kyu Cho has asserted his right under the Copyright, Designs and Patents Act, 1988 to be identified as the Author of this work.

British Library Cataloguing-in-Publication Data
A catalogue record for this book is available from the British Library

ISBN: 978-1-83973-627-8

Cover & Book Design: projectluz.com

To
Roberta, Isabella, and Rafael,
for the gift of living the story of salvation alongside you.

Contents

Part IV: From the Empty Tomb to the New Jerusalem

Foreword

For some years now in my speaking and writing, I have been in the habit of quoting from philosopher Alasdair MacIntyre's important book *After Virtue*: "I can only answer the question 'What am I to do?' if I can answer the prior question 'Of what story or stories do I find myself a part?'"[1] If we cannot answer this prior question, he proposes, then we shall find ourselves "unscripted, anxious stutterers"[2] in action as well as in word. It is a profound and important point about our human condition. Each of us "wakes up," as it were, in the midst of a story, whose beginning we only dimly remember, and whose precise ending we cannot predict. What is the true nature of this story? Is it a merely personal, individual narrative? Is it a slightly larger, but still only familial, or tribal, or national story? Or is there a still larger tale of which I find myself a part? On the answers to these questions hangs everything else – my sense of who I really am, where I should be heading, and how I should live.

The orthodox Christian answer to these questions involves a very large story indeed – the ultimately true story that makes sense of all other stories, true or false, ancient or contemporary. It is the story told in holy scripture, beginning in Genesis and ending in Revelation, and narrating at its center the birth, life, death, resurrection, and ascension of Jesus Christ. This Jesus himself looked back to the Old Testament, taking it as his own reference point for understanding the story in which he found himself. It was those truth-telling Scriptures, he taught, in whose context his truth (and his own person as Truth) was to be understood. They already revealed who God is, and who we are, and how we are to live. They already told of the one true God over against the many "gods" – the God who creates, out of love and not necessity, a world that bears his marks and knows his presence, but is not itself divine. These Old Testament Scriptures already told of human creatures designed for love for God and for all their creaturely neighbors – but endowed with freedom to express this love (or not). They already told of darkness, put under constraint by God in Genesis 1 so as to make it useful, but breaking free of its bonds in Genesis 3 and insinuating its way into human experience. They already told of all God's work to save this sinful and wounded world, not least through his

---

1. MacIntyre, *After Virtue*, 216.
2. Ibid.

chosen people Israel. They already foretold – these ancient Scriptures – a bright future for the cosmos, involving a Davidic king in whom the kingdom of God would arrive and all creation would be blessed. The Lord Jesus Christ is that King, entering the world first as Isaiah's suffering servant, but returning in our future as Daniel's glorious "son of man," and bringing in the new heaven and the new earth described in the Bible's closing chapters.

This is the story, claim the followers of Jesus Christ, of which all of us find ourselves a part – whether we know it yet or not. This is the story that makes sense of our human existence, as in faith we place our own personal, familial, tribal, and national stories within its context. This is the story that saves us from the fate of being "unscripted, anxious stutterers" in the world, lost in the cosmos and not knowing where to turn. "There is no tale ever told that men would rather find was true," J. R. R. Tolkien once said (in a 1939 lecture delivered at the University of St. Andrews in Scotland), "and none which so many skeptical men have accepted as true on its own merits. . . . To reject it leads either to sadness or to wrath."[3]

It is this wonderful, majestic, and true story that is the subject of the series of sermons found in this book – sermons on "Divine Presence, Human Vocation, and Cosmic Redemption." I recommend that you try not only to enjoy them (which will not be difficult), but also to *receive* them, as an invitation. To reject this story "leads either to sadness or to wrath." The invitation is rather to accept it, and thereby to find your rightful place in the world.

Iain Provan, PhD
Marshall Sheppard Professor of Biblical Studies,
Regent College, Canada

---

3. Tolkien, "Fairy Stories." This lecture (now entitled "On Fairy Stories") may now be found in *The Monsters and the Critics*, 109–61.

Acknowledgments

The core content of this book was originally produced in Portuguese, during the peak of the coronavirus pandemic in 2020, for a series of more than twenty sermons that I preached at Igreja Presbiteriana do Caminho, my home church in São Paulo. I hereby express my gratitude to the members of this community for being avid disciples of Jesus, and to my fellow leaders – Simon, Nata, Sae Won, Lendrão, Tche Paulo, Rachel, and Davi – for cultivating a fertile space for dialogue and mutual encouragement.

I am also grateful to my parents, Michael and Regina, for the constructive feedback they gave me throughout those months, and to my friend Ned Berube, who has been able to connect to our Sunday services via Zoom from his residence in Minnesota. Ned still calls me on a regular basis to remind me that it is indeed possible to lead a newly planted church in a pandemic, because the risen Christ – the only hero in the plot of salvation – has promised to walk with us until the end. I thank my fellow teacher at Seminário Teológico Servo de Cristo, Sandro Baggio, for speaking to our congregation on the missional character of the Christian vocation in October 2020. Some of his insights have been incorporated in the fourth part of this study. And my wife Roberta devoted long hours to reading what would eventually become the final manuscript of the original volume, thus helping me to shape the sermons into intelligible written texts.

Many thanks to Iain Provan for the elegant foreword above, which very helpfully sets the scene for what the reader will encounter in the following pages. Indeed, he and some other professors from Regent College are to blame for my understanding of the Bible as telling us a coherent, even if polyphonic, story (see Rikk Watts and Paul Williams in the footnotes). I thank as well Carmen Imes, Mariam Kovalishyn, Christopher Wright, and N. T. Wright for their generous endorsements. Chris, in particular, was prompt to recommend the publication of this English version with Langham Publishing, and Pieter Kwant was kind enough to accept the proposal. A special word of gratitude goes to Mark Arnold, Vivian Doub, and Luke Lewis, too, for facilitating the editorial process. Mark has given me some invaluable feedback on my English prose as well as on specific exegetical points. And I have to take this opportunity to thank – yet again – my Edinburgh *Doktorvater*, Matthew Novenson. Though I do not interact directly with his research here, Matt's scholarship and constant encouragement have been key sources of inspiration for my own (much more modest) effort as an author. Finally, a warm *obrigado* goes to the good people from Editora Mundo Cristão for first publishing the original material in Brazil: to Daniel Faria for his exceptional editorial work, as well as to Silvia Justino, Renato Fleischner, and Mark Carpenter for modeling competence and character in the essential task of providing resources for the body of Christ.

Why, to think of it, we're in the same tale still!
It's going on.
Don't the great tales never end?
– Samwise Gamgee[1]

1. Tolkien, *Lord of the Rings*, 712.

Introduction

Setting Up the Navigator

Almost twenty-five years ago, when I was finishing high school, a friend of mine asked me a very bewildering question: "Bernardo, if you died today, where would you go – heaven or hell?" The best response I could give was that I had never killed anyone, so my score would probably be (just) high enough to make the cut. In a veritable tour de force, my friend went on to spend a good forty minutes arguing that, despite my clean criminal record, the Bible said everyone was worthy of God's eternal judgment.

"Goodness, what must I do?" was my instant reply. My friend then pulled from his pocket a little yellow booklet titled *The Four Spiritual Laws*,[1] and from the very moment he told me about Jesus's death for my sins I was assured that I could live the rest of my life with a clear conscience. "You are saved, Bernardo. When you die, you will find your place in heaven. This is the wonderful plan God has reserved for you."

Without a shadow of a doubt, that conversation marked the beginning of a journey which four years later would culminate in the clear perception that I had been reached by Christ's saving grace. I must also admit that I know quite a few other people who have come to believe in the gospel by similar means. For some time after my first encounter with the "four spiritual laws," however, I would live with the conviction that the core of the biblical message had to do primarily with how human beings could secure their spot in heaven. To be "saved" was to be able to enjoy a relationship with God until the day he would "take" me from here.

But, as I started studying the Bible with the guidance of very smart people, it soon became clear to me that the gospel entails much broader realities than

---

1. First law: "God loves you and offers a wonderful plan for your life." Second law: "We are sinful and separated from God. Therefore, we cannot know and experience God's love and plan for our lives." Third law: "Jesus Christ is God's only provision for our sin. Through Him alone we can know God personally and experience God's love and plan." And the fourth law: "We must individually receive Jesus Christ as Savior and Lord; then we can know and experience God's love and plan for our lives." Source: www. https://knowgod.com/en/fourlaws/.

1

I had previously been taught. To my surprise, God's "wonderful plan" is not merely for "my life," but for the entire universe – the divine project is cosmic. Accordingly, God is interested not only in "having a relationship with me," but perhaps most importantly in fulfilling his purposes in the whole of creation. And the most shocking part was the realization that the story told in the Scriptures does not jump from the sin of Adam and Eve straight to Calvary. Jesus does not even show up in the first two thirds of the Bible: way before the birth of the Messiah, there is the calling of Abraham, the formation of Israel, the rule of the kings, the preaching of the prophets, the exile – and much more. And when Jesus himself does finally come onstage he teaches and does several important things before his death on the cross. All this, furthermore, before we even mention the crucial role the Holy Spirit plays in and through the disciples of Jesus, following his resurrection.

The point is simple: if we fail to grasp how the overarching plot of the Bible presents the core of its message, we inevitably reduce the gospel to something smaller than it actually is. And when that happens, the whole of our lives – our vision of God, our true identity as the chosen people in Christ, and our understanding of our place in the world – gets severely compromised. It is surely ironic that, even though my friend had convinced me to "accept Jesus in my heart," the gospel made very little difference in my life at that time. In the following years, I would continue to make all the poor choices that are typical of someone who cared little about "religion."

But the significance of this topic is not restricted to my private past. In the last couple decades, I have met a large number of people who, despite being born and raised in the church, struggle with a deep sense of disconnection between what they believe and the world around them. Some live as though Christianity is merely a mechanism to make them feel happy on Sundays, with no real relevance from Monday to Saturday. Moreover, who could have predicted that such a state of dislocation would come to the surface so dramatically in the pandemic that shook the planet in 2020? How many churchgoers have found themselves perplexed in the face of a virus that unveiled, among other things, the shallowness of their beliefs? In a situation like this, a skewed vision of the gospel – one which does not contemplate the totality of human existence – proves incapable of giving cohesion to life. As a result, many have either submitted to cheap conspiracy theories or given up calling themselves Christians altogether.

So what is it, after all, that the Bible tells us regarding God's "wonderful plan" for us and for the entire cosmos? What are the implications of the biblical message for the whole of our lives? Is it really the case that to be a Christian is merely to agree that Jesus died "for me" in order to secure my place "in heaven?"

In hopes of answering these questions, I decided to preach a series of sermons, starting in May 2020, focused on the unfolding of the story of salvation from Genesis to Revelation. Having finished a journey through the Sermon on the Mount, I realized that the members of my home church in São Paulo, recently affected by the "new normal" imposed by the coronavirus, needed to be reminded of the great biblical story in order to make sense again of their own stories in the world. And, after considering the possibility of shaping those sermons into a book, the board of Editora Mundo Cristão approved its publishing, which is now made available in English with Langham Publishing.

Divided into four sections comprising five chapters each – no parallels with the "four spiritual laws" intended! – the present volume covers what I regard as some of the main episodes of the history of salvation throughout the Scriptures. In the first part, we will examine the creation account, the fall, the call of Abraham, the exodus, and the formation of Israel. In the second part, we will give an overview from Sinai to the Babylonian captivity, discussing the golden calf incident, the time of the judges, the rules of David and Solomon, and then the exile. In the third part, we will cover the ministry of Jesus, examining the points of continuity with the story of his own people, his emphasis on the kingdom of God, his messianic and (surprisingly) divine identity, his victory over death, and the meaning of his resurrection. And, in the fourth part, we will discuss the mission of the church, paying particular attention to the Great Commission, the day of Pentecost, the reality of adoption by the Holy Spirit, the ministry of reconciliation, and the consummation of God's redemption in the New Jerusalem.

Since the present study is not a technical work, I have reduced the number of footnotes to a minimum, making use of them only in direct citations or when really indispensable. I have also avoided lingering in the minutiae of scholarly discussions, thus keeping my argument as fluid and accessible as possible. And, though the NRSV is the main English translation used here, my reading is always based on the original languages.

In terms of hermeneutical approach, the informed reader will notice that I take some well-defined starting points. First, I am persuaded that it is the biblical-theological categories – such as creation and new creation, exodus and new exodus, humanity and new humanity – that give coherence to some of the central emphases of the Scriptures. Second, the whole of a biblical book is as important as the sum of its parts, so attending to the cumulative force of its plot as well as to its ancient context is vital for grasping its meaning.

Third, the biblical canon presents an eschatological trajectory: from Genesis onwards, there is the expectation of a future, definitive resolution to the divine plan for the universe through humanity and, later on, the chosen people. And fourth, even though the Jewish Scriptures – known by Christians as the Old Testament – contrast with the New Testament in how they define some central concepts, the two Testaments are in full continuity with each other from the perspective of the overarching plot, the events in the latter being portrayed as the fulfillment of the former. This includes Jesus himself, who came "to fulfill" the "law and the prophets" (Matt 5:17).[2]

In short, far from being a collection of abstract propositions, the Bible gives us an account of how the Creator of the entire cosmos moved forward human history, himself entering the stage so as to reveal his character and redeem his creation. Should readers doubt this claim, they may ask Cleopas and his companion, who had to be reminded of some key elements of the biblical plot before realizing the presence of the risen Christ among them on the Emmaus Road (cf. Luke 24:13–35).[3] So, while the Bible contains a variety of books in different genres addressing various historical concerns, not only does it tell a story predominantly in narrative form, but also this very same story is often implicit across the canon.[4]

My aim, therefore, is to recalibrate our understanding of what it means to be the people of God in the light of the story of salvation told in the Scriptures.

---

2. For brevity, I here give credit to my foremost conversation partners, whose research has in many ways broken the ground for my effort in this book: Alter, *Biblical Narrative*; Bartholomew and Goheen, *Drama of Scripture*; Bauckham, *Gospel of Glory*; Beale, *Church's Mission*; Beale, *Teologia Bíblica* [*Biblical Theology*]; Beale and Kim, *Deus Mora entre Nós* [*God Dwells among Us*]; Brueggemann, *Theology of the Old Testament*; Childs, *Biblical Theology*; Cullmann, *Christology of the New Testament*; Hays, *Gospels*; Hays, *Letters of Paul*; Hooker, "Who Can This Be?"; Imes, *Bearing God's Name*; Juel, *Messianic Exegesis*; Kingsbury, *Matthew as Story*; Kirschner, "Nova Jerusalém"; Provan, *Seriously Dangerous Religion*; Provan, Long, and Longman III, *Biblical History*; Von Rad, *Old Testament Theology*; Walton, *Ancient Near Eastern Thought*; Walton, *Adam and Eve*; Watts, *New Exodus in Mark*; C. J. H. Wright, *Mission of God*; Wright, *Old Testament Ethics*; Wright, *Seven Sentences*; N. T. Wright, *Victory of God*; Wright, *People of God*; Yarbro Collins, "Mark and His Readers." I should also mention a course taught by Rikk Watts during my final years at Regent College, titled "It's about Life."

3. At this point, I must clarify that this book does not provide a systematic manual on soteriology, missiology, or eschatology. In the following pages, the reader will not find any extensive treatment on the various theories of atonement, for example, nor do I spend much time grappling with whatever will immediately precede the return of Christ.

4. This is not to say that there is only one way to explain the rich and admittedly polyphonic content of the Bible, nor is it to dismiss the importance of investigating the historical origins of each of its parts. It is simply to follow the kind of reading adopted by biblical authors such as Paul, who thought that God's interventions in history followed a consistent pattern "in accordance with the scriptures" (cf. 1 Cor 15:3).

As my former teacher Iain Provan has reminded us in the foreword, all of us are part of a larger narrative – whether we recognize it or not. One of the underestimated heroes of the *Lord of the Rings* trilogy, Samwise Gamgee, to whom I owe this book's epigraph, came to realize precisely this fact at a critical junction of his mission alongside Frodo Baggins.[5] In other words, *The Plot of Salvation* seeks to adjust the lenses through which we see all things, so that our perspective of the scope of the redemption in Christ – and, consequently, of our whole lives – might be expanded.[6] As we journey through the plot of salvation, I hope you, the reader, will be reminded that Jesus's lordship touches every single corner of the cosmos created by God.[7]

---

5. For a more detailed treatment of the importance of stories to our self-understanding, see Provan, 1–20, who also cites Samwise Gamgee's saying to illustrate his point.

6. I owe this illustration to Paul Williams. See Williams, "Reframing Story," the first episode of an excellent ten-video resource available at ReFrame, https://www.reframecourse.com.

7. My unpretentious paraphrase of Abraham Kuyper's famous thesis. See Bratt, *Abraham Kuyper*, 488.

Part I

From Creation to Israel

1

In the Beginning, God "Formed" and "Filled": Creation as Sacred Space

In the beginning when God created the heavens and the earth, the earth was a formless void and darkness covered the face of the deep, while a wind from God swept over the face of the waters. . . .

Thus the heavens and the earth were finished, and all their multitude. And on the seventh day God finished the work that he had done, and he rested on the seventh day from all the work that he had done. So God blessed the seventh day and hallowed it, because on it God rested from all the work that he had done in creation. (Gen 1:1–2; 2:1–3)

My apologies to fans of J. R. R. Tolkien, but I must confess that it took me a while to enjoy the *Lord of the Rings* trilogy. I did find the world of Middle-earth fascinating, and the beauty of the script is very hard to deny. The reason is slightly more embarrassing, at least for me. Since I was unfamiliar with the original novels when the movies were released, I simply didn't get all the hype. Having been born into a family of Korean immigrants in Brazil, I became aware of the wealth of English literature only in my early adulthood. And on the three occasions when I tried to follow the screen version of the adventures of Frodo Baggins and Samwise Gamgee, each time something unexpected would happen to prevent me from catching the beginning of the story. When I would finally take a seat, the Fellowship of the Ring had already been formed, and the only thing I could think of was, "Why, for goodness' sake, should a golden ring cause such hassle to those hobbits?" (I should also mention that none of my co-viewers ever cared to explain to me the parts that I had missed.)

It was only a few years ago, when I finally set myself to watch the trilogy alone, and hence with complete freedom to "rewind the tape" if necessary, that all those pieces finally came together. The key was in the first minutes of the movie: in the ancient, mythical universe imagined by Tolkien, a golden ring had been forged to give almost infinite powers to whoever possessed it. Life and death, then, depended on the success of the mission entrusted to Frodo and Sam. They were to journey all the way to Mount Doom, the only place where said ring could be destroyed, so as to throw the object in the fires therein. The overall story is obviously much more complex than I have just described, but the point is that I was only able to understand it when I managed to comprehend its opening scenes. In the world of narratives, the beginnings are always programmatic.

The Christian message was passed down to us predominantly in the form of stories. And, to the surprise of many, the biblical plot does not begin with Jesus. Without him, to be sure, we would still wander in disorientation, ignorant of the ultimate realities to which the Scriptures point, dead in our sins. As much as the good news is revealed fully and definitively in Jesus, however, he himself is part of a larger story that begins long before his birth. Our message begins at the starting point of the entire cosmos: "In the beginning . . . God created the heavens and the earth."

What follows is that to see clearly the theological thrust of the creation account is essential not only for the Old Testament scholar, but for anyone who seeks to make sense of what Jesus accomplished in his life, death, and resurrection. One of the most prolific early Christian authors, the apostle Paul, would certainly agree with this statement. In his exposition of the gospel in Athens, the apostle builds precisely upon the same scriptural claim:

> The God who made the world and everything in it is the Lord of heaven and earth and does not live in temples built by human hands. And he is not served by human hands, as if he needed anything. Rather, he himself gives everyone life and breath and everything else. (Acts 17:24–25)

Unfortunately, the creation account in Genesis has been used, by some at least, almost exclusively in combat with secular versions of evolutionary theory that deny God's creative activity. Such apologetic interests are indeed necessary at times, but we also must beware of the risks of reading the text differently to the way the literary genre deployed by the inspired author should guide our interpretation. Simply put, respecting the parameters of the text itself, far from diminishing the authority of Scripture, helps us to see the biblical message more accurately.

Most scholars agree that the purpose of Genesis 1–2 is to tell us *who* created the world and *for what purpose*, rather than to provide a scientific treatment of *how* the universe came to be. Its poetic, almost liturgical tone[1] suggests that a concern much broader than mere chemical processes is in view. Consider the following excerpt:

> Then God said, "Let there be light"; and there was light. And God saw that the light was good; and God separated the light from the darkness. God called the light Day, and the darkness he called Night. And there was evening and there was morning, the first day.
>
> And God said, "Let there be a dome in the midst of the waters, and let it separate the waters from the waters." So God made the dome and separated the waters that were under the dome from the waters that were above the dome. And it was so. God called the dome Sky. And there was evening and there was morning, the second day.
>
> And God said, "Let the waters under the sky be gathered together into one place, and let the dry land appear." And it was so. God called the dry land Earth, and the waters that were gathered together he called Seas. And God saw that it was good. Then God said, "Let the earth put forth vegetation: plants yielding seed, and fruit trees of every kind on earth that bear fruit with the seed in it." And it was so. The earth brought forth vegetation: plants yielding seed of every kind, and trees of every kind bearing fruit with the seed in it. And God saw that it was good. And there was evening and there was morning, the third day. (Gen 1:3–13)

Indeed, the use of repetition – "God said: 'Let there be . . . ,'" "And there was . . . ," "God saw that it was good," and "there was evening and there was morning" – goes on till the end of the chapter (cf. Gen 1:31), and recalls the pattern of some of the songs we sing at our Sunday services.

What, then, is the main point of Genesis 1–2? That the biblical author borrowed imagery from a thought world that was common to his contemporaries is clear from the statement that "the Spirit of God was hovering over the waters"

---

1. See discussion in Brueggemann, *Genesis*, 29–36.

(NIV).[2] These waters are most likely a reference to the primeval waters from which the people in the Ancient Near East believed the world was made.

But, in contrast to those commonly held myths, Genesis 1:1 also says that "God created the heavens and the earth." Particularly in Mesopotamia, it was believed that the universe had resulted from a complicated series of interactions between the entities of chaos and the gods of order, the heavenly bodies themselves being regarded as somewhat divine. The Babylonian text *Enuma Elish* provides us with some important information on this. The biblical God, on the other hand, both creates everything by the simple act of speaking and establishes order within the cosmos by his free initiative. This is the same God who would eventually reveal himself to Israel as YHWH. So, in clear discontinuity with the neighboring worldviews, Genesis 1–2 claims that the cosmos is neither divine nor accidental. All things in the heavens and in the earth ultimately owe their existence to the one Creator, who is to be thoroughly distinguished from his creatures.

In addition, we are told that "the earth was a formless void [*tōhû wābōhû*]." This is crucial for our understanding of what comes next, because everything that God does on the six days of creation happens "to form" and "to fill" the universe, thus solving its "formless and empty" (NIV) condition. On the first three days, God gives shape to the universe by separating light from darkness, waters from waters, and waters from land. And, from the second half of the third day onwards, God creates everything that fills the heavens and the earth: the vegetation, the sun, the moon, and the animals. A very important aspect of this process, moreover, is the fact that God gives each element of the cosmos a function. The "lights," for example, were positioned in "the sky" in order to "rule" the day and the night as well as to "separate the light from the darkness," and the animals were to be "fruitful and multiply." The basic fact that God not only filled and formed the earth, but also assigned a task to each of its parts, makes the theological point that the universe was created for a specific purpose: as a wise and creative architect who designs an exquisite dwelling place, he provides the universe with structure and all the conditions for the flourishing of life.

There is one detail in Genesis 1–2, however, that should puzzle readers, especially if they are familiar with what the ancient peoples believed about their gods and the world.[3] Something that had paramount importance in any culture around that time, and yet is completely absent in the creation account, was a

---

2. An excellent introduction is found in Longman, *How to Read Genesis*.

3. See Walton, *Ancient Near Eastern Thought*, 73–96; and Provan, 32–33.

temple. This is highly significant, given that temples were micro-representations of the universe and served as points of intersection between human existence and the divine realm. Until recent times, temples have occupied the most central place in any society precisely for this reason. In short, a temple was the resting place of a deity – its "official residence," where the god took its seat – from which dominion over a particular sphere was exercised.

And, strikingly, though no temple is mentioned in Genesis 1–2, nevertheless the text says that God "rested" – from the Hebrew *shavat* – on the seventh day. In other words, having "formed" and "filled" the cosmos, the Creator acted as though he had a temple. But where exactly did he sit to "rest"?

This is where the importance of the seventh day comes to the surface. In the ancient world, the pagan temples functioned as the resting places of the deities, from which said deities exercised dominion over the realities pertaining to them. The temples, that is, were the "official residences" of the so-called gods. Moreover, the fact that God himself "rests" on the seventh day also alludes to the image of a sacred space. In the thought world of Genesis 1–2, it was common for the consecration of a sanctuary to take seven days.[4] The famous temple of Solomon was no exception to this rule (cf. 1 Kgs 8:65).

Now, the biblical God is all-powerful, fully able to create all things at once, in the blink of an eye. Why bother spending seven twenty-four-hour days to do something that could be achieved in much less time? The answer is that, in speaking of the origins of the universe in terms of God's forming and filling the earth, giving the cosmos a specific purpose, and finally resting on the seventh day, the biblical text is saying that the world was designed to be God's own sacred space. In Paul's words, after all, "the God who made the world and everything in it, he who is Lord of heaven and earth, does not live in shrines made by human hands" (Acts 17:24). Accordingly, Genesis 1–2 further subverts competing worldviews by presenting the cosmos as the place where the loving care of the Creator was to be made tangible, without the need for a temple. God created the universe to make himself available in it and to govern the heavens and the earth by his perfect will.

That said, we should mention another key idea presented in Genesis 1–2. If God created the cosmos in order to dwell in it and exercise his rule over it, how would this happen in concrete terms? Again, in the ancient world, the last element to be installed inside a temple was the image of the deity, as its representation. Significantly, what the Creator does on the sixth day, before resting on the seventh day, is to make humanity in his "image and likeness":

---

4. Walton, 73–96; Provan, 32–33.

Then God said, "Let us make humankind in our image, according to our likeness; and let them have dominion over the fish of the sea, and over the birds of the air, and over the cattle, and over all the wild animals of the earth, and over every creeping thing that creeps upon the earth."

So God created humankind in his image,
    in the image of God he created them;
    male and female he created them.

God blessed them, and God said to them, "Be fruitful and multiply, and fill the earth and subdue it; and have dominion over the fish of the sea and over the birds of the air and over every living thing that moves upon the earth." (Gen 1:26–28)

As bearers of God's image, human beings are to be his regents by keeping the cosmos as his sacred space. It is precisely this reality that is envisaged in Eden: Adam and Eve receive the task to cultivate God's garden and thus to embody his wisdom (cf. Gen 2:4–25). And note the emphasis: all "humankind" (*'āḏām*) – that is, "male and female" – was given that identity and called for that purpose.

The implications of Genesis 1–2 are huge. In the light of this programmatic vision, it is imperative that Christians reject some pagan myths of our own time which claim that the world is nothing more than a pool of resources to be explored or essentially an evil place from which it is supposedly best for us to depart. We must also resist much of contemporary political discourse that measures human dignity according to nationality, race, social location, or gender. As soon as we deviate from the biblical picture of the cosmos as God's temple and of all human beings as his image bearers, we fall prey to ideas that are necessarily reductionistic, idolatrous, and potentially harmful. Worse yet: to ignore the theological vision of the creation account will eventually prevent us from understanding the gospel itself.

This is the problem with thinking that the world is irreversibly doomed, and this is why the New Testament makes it impossible for us to suppose that all that Jesus offers his disciples is a chance to go somewhere else after they die. People who hold these views are like myself some years ago trying to make sense of the *Lord of the Rings* with absolutely no regard to the beginning of the film. By making the wrong assumption that the world is bad and disposable, they have lost sight of the most basic truth in the story, thus becoming unable to grasp clearly the end as well. As Iain Provan puts it:

The world that is created by the personal God is therefore never regarded by biblical faith as a problem to be overcome. It is good. There are problems that arise *within* the world, to be sure. *These* must be overcome. The world itself, however, is not a problem to be overcome.[5]

It is no surprise then that, if the opening chapters of the Bible claim all these things, its conclusion culminates in God's new creation, where he will dwell permanently with his resurrected people (cf. Rev 21–22).

And the portrayal of humanity at the highest point in this divine project reveals our ultimate vocation. We were made to worship the Creator, to express his character, and to mediate his gracious rule to all creatures. Not to live according to this vision is to fall short of our humanity and to be entangled in what Charles Taylor has described as the deepest of all identity crises.[6]

This then is the beginning of the story. God created the heavens and the earth so that he might inhabit the cosmos as his temple. And God created human beings so that they would represent him in the universe, enjoying the whole of life with him. This is why, throughout this process, Genesis 1–2 repeatedly states that God saw that it was "good" (*ṭôḇ*) – and, at the end, "very good" (*ṭôḇ meʼōḏ*). Let us join the psalmist and declare: "The heavens declare the glory of God; the skies proclaim the work of his hands" (Ps 19:1 NIV).

---

5. Provan, 41 (emphases original).

6. Taylor, *Ethics of Authenticity*.

2

Distrust, Rupture, and Death: The Installation of Chaos through the Fall

Now the serpent was more crafty than any other wild animal that the LORD God had made. He said to the woman, "Did God say, 'You shall not eat from any tree in the garden'?" The woman said to the serpent, "We may eat of the fruit of the trees in the garden; but God said, 'You shall not eat of the fruit of the tree that is in the middle of the garden, nor shall you touch it, or you shall die.'" But the serpent said to the woman, "You will not die; for God knows that when you eat of it your eyes will be opened, and you will be like God, knowing good and evil." So when the woman saw that the tree was good for food, and that it was a delight to the eyes, and that the tree was to be desired to make one wise, she took of its fruit and ate; and she also gave some to her husband, who was with her, and he ate. (Gen 3:1–6)

As we saw in the previous chapter, God called the universe "very good," providing for it all that was needed for the flourishing of life. But this certainly does not mean that the cosmos was incorruptible or unconditionally perfect. In fact, every single day – not least in times of political crisis and financial instability occasioned by a global pandemic – we are reminded that the world, albeit beautiful, is fragile and often extremely dangerous. To borrow an image from C. S. Lewis, the universe expresses the brilliance of the most excellent Artist, while at the same time reflecting the presence of very cruel forces.[1] And this is true not only when it comes to the world itself, but most importantly regarding humanity. We are the most sublime creatures among the living beings on earth, but we are also the main source of its decadence – our own and creation's decadence alike. What could possibly explain such lack of symmetry between the picture of Genesis 1–2 and our own experience?

Before we answer that question, it is helpful to understand that, when God created the universe and appointed humanity as his representatives, the cosmos existed in a state of order, not of consummation. As biblical scholar G. K. Beale notes, the creation account represents the beginning of a project intended to point forward to a glorious climax.[2] In this regard, the garden of Eden was not meant primarily to function as some sort of five-star resort, but rather as a sacred space to be preserved: the earth was to be cultivated by humanity. To be made in the image of God was therefore, among other things, to be given the grace of participating in God's continuous work of taking his creation to its ultimate climax. This is what seems to be implicit in the words of Psalm 8:6: "You have given them dominion over the works of your hands; you have put all things under their feet."

I like to illustrate this point by thinking of how my daughter first became a junior baker. In her first attempts, my wife and I would call our parents to show them the "amazing" cakes our then three-year-old Isabella had just baked. But all of us knew that, by saying "Isabella made a cake," we actually meant that she held the bowl while her parents mixed the dough and did everything else. All of the ingredients had been chosen by my wife, and the little girl simply took part in minor details of the process.

This is more or less what is envisaged in Genesis 1–2: God had ordered the cosmos so that humanity could fulfill their vocation of keeping the world as a sacred space where the Creator could dwell with them forever. It is surely instructive, then, that God places Adam in the garden of Eden in order for him to do a specific work: "The LORD God took the man and put him in the garden of Eden to till it and keep it" (Gen 2:15). This goal, however, could be achieved only insofar as humanity retained the Creator as their absolute point of reference. Not only would humanity constantly need God's guidance to fulfill their vocation in the cosmos, but also the order of the universe depended on humanity's faithfully mediating God's presence in his cosmic temple. Stated differently, in order for the cosmos to reach its fullness through the creatures

---

1. Lewis, *Cristianismo Puro e Simples* [*Mere Christianity*], 40.
2. Beale, *Teologia Bíblica*, 47–69.

made in the Creator's image, humanity needed to remain committed to their fundamental purpose of relying on God's wisdom and expressing it in all things.

It is at this point that we need to note what happens to the first couple mentioned in the Bible – Adam and Eve:

> And the LORD God planted a garden in Eden, in the east; and there he put the man whom he had formed. Out of the ground the LORD God made to grow every tree that is pleasant to the sight and good for food, the tree of life also in the midst of the garden, and the tree of the knowledge of good and evil. . . .
>
> The LORD God took the man and put him in the garden of Eden to till it and keep it. And the LORD God commanded the man, "You may freely eat of every tree of the garden; but of the tree of the knowledge of good and evil you shall not eat, for in the day that you eat of it you shall die."
>
> Then the LORD God said, "It is not good that the man should be alone; I will make him a helper as his partner." . . . So the LORD God caused a deep sleep to fall upon the man, and he slept; then he took one of his ribs and closed up its place with flesh. And the rib that the LORD God had taken from the man he made into a woman and brought her to the man. (Gen 2:8–9, 15–18, 21–22)

Adam and Eve are important because they are the ones who received the very specific task of being the first representatives of the human race. The precise relation between the couple in Genesis 2 and humanity in general in Genesis 1:26–27 still seems to be a matter of scholarly dispute, but the relevance of Adam and Eve for the future of the entire cosmos is beyond question. When the Bible affirms that God formed the first significant couple and appointed them as guardians of the garden of Eden, something vital is being said: they were to play the crucial role of leading the entire human species in the work of keeping the cosmos as God's sacred space – something like the eventual relationship between the high priest and the other Levites. And the aim was to expand the reality of the divine presence beyond the garden of Eden, to the ends of the earth. In brief, Adam and Eve were the first among equals, the captains of the team, who were to head humanity in their original vocation. (Paul will take this point for granted in his comparison of Christ with Adam in Rom 5:12–21.)

This explains why Genesis 2 describes the task of Adam and Eve fundamentally in terms of a stance they should take towards two specific trees – namely, "the tree of life" and "the tree of the knowledge of good and evil."

Tree imagery figured prominently in the ancient world, and here likely refers figuratively to the source of one's subsistence.[3] God's making those two trees grow at the center of Eden, then, indicates that Adam and Eve are presented with two contrasting paths of existence, two distinct ways of life. On the one hand, "the tree of life" symbolizes the human vocation to depend on God's wisdom, to live in communion with him, and thus to keep the cosmos as his sacred dwelling place. Hence the name "the tree of life": everlasting life with the eternal Creator in the place he had designed to be his temple. On the other hand, "the tree of the knowledge of good and evil," as its name suggests, stands for the opposite: to decide for themselves, with no regard to God's wisdom, what constitutes "good" and "evil." The forbidden tree, that is, represents the possibility of living independently from the Creator. Hence the result of eating from this tree: "in the day that you eat of it you shall die." To follow the path of the autonomous knowledge of good and evil is to take God out of the equation, rejecting his character as the ultimate point of reference. And the most obvious consequence of this choice would be the inexorability of death itself – the final expression of alienation from the divine presence and the entering of chaos into the cosmos.

But this raises a few questions. If God so desired to dwell in his cosmic home, why in the world did he make room for that also not to happen? What is more, why did he place the forbidden tree alongside the good tree, at the center of the garden? Why not conceal the former among the thorny bushes? (Sometimes, my wife and I have to take extreme measures and hide the chocolate underneath the broccoli so that our kids don't eat it all.)

Indeed, these issues have puzzled even the most brilliant minds in the history of the church, but we may underscore a couple of points for our purposes. We must never lose sight of the fact that God created humanity in his image and likeness, not to be programmable machines. This means that Adam and Eve were able, among many other things, to love and to obey the Creator. Love and obedience, however, are legitimate only insofar as they are voluntary. Free love always entails the possibility of responding otherwise. And the same goes with genuine obedience. The fact that God granted Adam and Eve an alternative to a life of dependance on his wisdom, therefore, indicates that he took the human vocation very seriously. The Creator did not pretend to make humanity in his image and likeness: by giving Adam and Eve the possibility of living autonomously, he took the risk of someone who truly loves. By the same token, God's placing of the forbidden tree in the middle of

---

3. Walton, Matthews, and Chavalas, *Old Testament*, 31.

the garden also envisaged humanity's protection. If the order of the cosmos should be maintained through Adam and Eve's dependance on the Creator's knowledge of "good and evil," the two trees would remind them precisely of this: the harmony of the cosmos hinged on the fundamental purpose for humanity to reject autonomy and to worship God.

God's prohibition of eating from "the tree of the knowledge of good and evil" must be heard in the context of his affirmation of the goodness of creation and the sublime purpose for which humanity had been created. Some readers tend to emphasize the negative aspect of the divine order – "you shall not eat" – but, in fact, the text gives us an altogether different tone. Before even forbidding Adam from eating of that one particular tree – to be precise, Eve had not been "made" prior to Genesis 2:21 – God gives him access to the rest of the garden in its entirety: "You may freely eat of *every* tree of the garden" (2:16, emphasis added). This underscores the key point that the commandments in Genesis 2:17 are aimed at preserving human freedom in the light of the divine generosity. The injunction not to follow the path of moral independence comes from God's desire to prevent humanity submitting themselves to alienation and death.

With these ideas in mind, we are now in the position to understand what is at stake in the event traditionally known as "the fall." In brief, Genesis 3 explains how sin entered the world and occasioned the mismatch between the original state of creation and most of the evil we experience to this day. But what exactly was the fall, and why did it cause such a mess in the cosmos, previously regarded by God himself as very good?

Though we often forget this, before sin was actualized in the transgression of the divine commandment, it was rooted in humanity's distrust of the goodness of God. In the biblical account, when the serpent approaches Eve, instead of "forcing" her into disobeying God, it actually poses a question about the Creator's words: "Did God say, 'You shall not eat from any tree in the garden'?" (Gen 3:1). (In the ancient world, serpent imagery could represent chaos or order, depending on the context.[4] In the thought world of Genesis, the serpent represents the forces which Adam and Eve should have subdued, in consonance with their vocation as the divine regents in the cosmos.) The important thing to note here is the subtlety of the temptation: not only does the serpent stress the negative aspect of God's prohibition, but it also distorts what he had actually said – the Creator had forbidden humanity's taking from *one* specific place, not from *any* tree in the garden.

---

4. Walton, Matthews, and Chavalas, 31–32.

Eve, then, buys into such a false emphasis and as a result misrepresents – or, better, gives her own slightly exaggerated version of – the limits imposed by the Creator: "God said, 'You shall not eat of the fruit of the tree that is in the middle of the garden, nor shall you *touch* it, or you shall die'" (Gen 3:3, emphasis added). We thus have to agree with John Calvin and Dietrich Bonhoeffer when they point out that Eve's failure accurately to interpret the divine words is the reason behind her falling short of holding on to them.[5] At this point, the reader is also left wondering whether Adam was faithful in relaying to Eve what they were supposed (and not supposed) to do. The text says nothing about this, but the fact that the former ends up likewise eating the fruit may suggest this prior problem.

Once Eve takes the bait, the serpent proceeds to convince her that the "real" reason God told them not to take from "the tree of the knowledge of good and evil" was that he was afraid that humanity would become "like him." According to the tempter, God was insecure and self-absorbed: "You will not die; for God knows that when you eat of it your eyes will be opened, and you will be like God, knowing good and evil" (Gen 3:4–5). In other words, "Oh, don't believe a word this God says, for the truth is that you will have his absolute knowledge the moment you eat from this tree. The Creator may seem awesome. . . . In reality, though, he is just a selfish tyrant. You need to break free from his bondage. Eat the fruit and be like him." (The implicit irony here, of course, is that, having been created in God's image and likeness, humanity was already "like him" in the proper sense of the term.) At the center of the first sin, therefore, is the undermining of humanity's trust in the goodness of God.

What follows from this deceit is that, all of a sudden, Eve notices the "delightful" aspect of the forbidden tree and finds the possibility of becoming like God, without having to rely on him, very compelling indeed. She takes the fruit, and as the final straw Adam eats it too, in an irreversible neglect of God's command.

It is this that explains the discrepancy between the vision of Genesis 1–2 and much of reality surrounding us: sin entered the world when humanity lost sight of the character of the Creator, rebelling against his will, thinking it possible to be like God without him. The fall was Adam and Eve's attempt at ascending to God's position, which led them to forfeit their fundamental vocation and to dig their own grave. Consequently, as soon as humanity decided to live according to their own understanding of "good and evil," the harmony of the cosmos began to be severely disrupted. And, from humanity's very

---

5. See Calvin, *Institutes* II.1.4; and Bonhoeffer, *Temptation*.

conscience regarding their identity in relation to the Creator, the distortions caused by sin soon spread out horizontally to all areas of reality:

> Then the eyes of both were opened, and they knew that they were naked; and they sewed fig leaves together and made loincloths for themselves.
>
> They heard the sound of the LORD God walking in the garden at the time of the evening breeze, and the man and his wife hid themselves from the presence of the LORD God among the trees of the garden. But the LORD God called to the man, and said to him, "Where are you?" He said, "I heard the sound of you in the garden, and I was afraid, because I was naked; and I hid myself." He said, "Who told you that you were naked? Have you eaten from the tree of which I commanded you not to eat?" The man said, "The woman whom you gave to be with me, she gave me fruit from the tree, and I ate." Then the LORD God said to the woman, "What is this that you have done?" The woman said, "The serpent tricked me, and I ate." The LORD God said to the serpent,

> "Because you have done this,
>   cursed are you among all animals
>   and among all wild creatures;
> upon your belly you shall go,
>   and dust you shall eat
>   all the days of your life.
> I will put enmity between you and the woman,
>   and between your offspring and hers;
> he will strike your head,
>   and you will strike his heel."

To the woman he said,

> "I will greatly increase your pangs in childbearing;
>   in pain you shall bring forth children,
> yet your desire shall be for your husband,
>   and he shall rule over you."

And to the man he said,

> "Because you have listened to the voice of your wife,
>   and have eaten of the tree

about which I commanded you,
>   'You shall not eat of it,'
cursed is the ground because of you;
>   in toil you shall eat of it all the days of your life;
thorns and thistles it shall bring forth for you;
>   and you shall eat the plants of the field.
By the sweat of your face
>   you shall eat bread
until you return to the ground,
>   for out of it you were taken;
you are dust,
>   and to dust you shall return." (Gen 3:7–19)

Because God is no longer Adam and Eve's point of reference, humanity immediately attributes shame to their nudity. Moreover, not only do they alienate themselves from each other – Adam blames Eve – but a high degree of estrangement arises between them and the rest of creation. Their labor becomes burdensome, and suffering is from that point on their lasting companion. But worst of all: the unity of heaven and earth, which holds together God's cosmic temple, suffers a rupture, so that the Creator himself cannot dwell among humanity as he originally did before sin. It is almost as though sin has so compromised the health of the cosmos that, in Genesis 3, the divine presence and humanity must be put in quarantine.

In sum, the fall results in the tragic reality that God's cosmic temple has to stay, in some significant sense, uninhabited. Adam and Eve are driven out of the garden of Eden, access to "the tree of life" is blocked, and chaos ensues:

> Then the LORD God said, "See, the man has become like one of us, knowing good and evil; and now, he might reach out his hand and take also from the tree of life, and eat, and live forever" – therefore the LORD God sent him forth from the garden of Eden, to till the ground from which he was taken. He drove out the man; and at the east of the garden of Eden he placed the cherubim, and a sword flaming and turning to guard the way to the tree of life. (Gen 3:22–24)

It is in Genesis 3, therefore, that we discover the roots of our main sores. Humanity preferred independence from God and thus submitted themselves to death. And every single one of us, without exception, follows in the footsteps of Adam and Eve. This is one of the most easily demonstrable facts of life. Look, for example, at our many identity crises and insecurities, as well as at our propensity for nihilism, idolatry, injustice, war, oppression, and abuse of creation. Far from being the mere outcome of chance or of corrupted social structures, then, the chaos with which we are all too familiar has its origin in the human desire to be "like God." Humanity alienated themselves from the Creator. This is our problem.

3

One Family, Blessing to All: God's Promise to Abraham

Now the LORD said to Abram, "Go from your country and your kindred and your father's house to the land that I will show you. I will make of you a great nation, and I will bless you, and make your name great, so that you will be a blessing. I will bless those who bless you, and the one who curses you I will curse; and in you all the families of the earth shall be blessed." (Gen 12:1–3)

If we were to follow the basic outline some churchgoers still use to summarize the Christian message, the present chapter should have been devoted to presenting an exposition of how Jesus "stamps our passports" to heaven through his death at Calvary. To the surprise of many, however, the Bible does not skip from Genesis 3 to Mark 15.

Sin seriously affected the condition of the human soul, and the episodes after the fall of Adam and Eve tell us of the divine plan to redeem the very good cosmos in its entirety, not only our individual consciences. Human autonomy has had deeply degenerative consequences for how things work in the world. This means that it will take a long while for the cosmic harmony to be reestablished and for God's holy presence to dwell fully among his creatures once again. The cosmos, after all, is unable to develop antibodies to the virus of our alienation from the Creator, and the quarantine between humanity and God could not be relaxed so rapidly. So the fall does not find an immediate resolution, because it is impossible for the restoration of heaven and earth to take place by means of a simple process.

A related problem is that, in order for the malady initiated by Adam and Eve to be remedied, it would be necessary to deal with the real source of the disease, not only the symptoms. Chaos and death must be dealt with from their roots. And, as we saw in the previous chapter, the fundamental cause of the fall was that humanity decided to reject the divine wisdom as the path of life and to live autonomously from the Creator. Accordingly, sin has placed us in a kind of cul-de-sac. How could the effects of the fall be reversed if humanity turned their backs in rebellion on the only way possible for the cosmos to reach its climactic goal – namely, the possibility to grow into the knowledge of God and fellowship with him? And how could those following in the footsteps of Adam and Eve learn to depend on the Creator, if the fall caused separation from him?

We notice, then, that the redemption of the universe entails the recovery of humanity's vocation, which in turn requires the resumption of their relationship with God. The problem, though, is that, in the context where human beings already know the taste of independence and thus find themselves in the dark concerning the life of the Creator, such a recovery would be possible only if God himself unveiled his character and goodness in history. There could be no shortcuts.

Hence, we don't see a Hollywood-style happy ending in Genesis 4. Rather, we witness the concrete effects of sin not only on the first significant couple of the biblical narrative, but on everyone who lives on the face of the earth. That which God had announced in Genesis 3 indeed takes place, with no delay. In a world created by someone who is perfectly good and at the same time absolutely just, every human act has consequences. And the outcome of the disobedience of Adam and Eve is seen particularly in the trajectory into which sin leads humanity: a downward spiral, ever more distant from the vision of Eden. The subsequent chapters, therefore, make it abundantly clear that alienation and brokenness, which entered the cosmos in Genesis 3, became the inescapable experiences of every single person in the world.

It is indicative that the first story after the expulsion from the garden of Eden is the famous episode in which Cain murders his own brother, Abel (Gen 4:1–16). The passage is filled with dark and intriguing details, but what matters for our purposes is Cain's response when God asks him about his (dead) brother: "Am I my brother's keeper?" (4:9). What a distance from the vision of Genesis 1–2! Furthermore, in Genesis 6, some figures called "sons of God" decide to "take" some women by force, as if these were mere possessions.[1]

---

1. The identity of the "sons of God" in Gen 6:1–4 is hotly debated, but I take the view that the expression refers to powerful men who took women by force. See Walton, Matthews, and Chavalas, *Old Testament*, 36.

It is not terribly surprising that such a trajectory finds its climax in the flood. What is the flood if not a sort of return of the earth to the tyranny of chaos? In Genesis 1:2, before God starts "to form" and "to fill" the heavens and the earth, the Spirit of the Creator fluttered over the "waters." As previously pointed out, these "waters" represent the pre-orderly state of creation. In pouring out his judgment through the flood, in other words, God hands humanity over to the consequences of the evil they have been practicing since Genesis 4.

And even after Noah and his family are protected, by God's unilateral initiative, from that catastrophe, that precarious state of affairs does not seem to change. Even though Noah is famous for his obedience to God, not least in his building of the ark wherein the partial order of the cosmos would be moved forward, humanity resumed their pursuit of autonomy as soon as the earth was dry. The building of the tower of Babel is the most emblematic event of this kind: "Then they said, 'Come, let us build ourselves a city, and a tower with its top in the heavens, and let us make a name for ourselves; otherwise we shall be scattered abroad upon the face of the whole earth'" (Gen 11:4). The result, again, is confusion and dispersion. When we reach the end of Genesis 11, it is transparent that human beings are incapable of regenerating themselves – they cannot produce the antibodies for the virus called sin.

And yet, the biblical account shows us that human failure is only one component of the whole picture. While it is true that the fall damaged the order of the cosmos, Genesis depicts the Creator in constant movement toward humanity: God approaches Cain to persuade him to "do well" and to "master sin" (Gen 4:7), and shows his unmerited "favor" to Noah prior to his building of the ark (6:8).[2] The genealogies presented thus far in the narrative also indicate the same reality. An important theological function of the genealogies in the biblical literature is to make the point that God insists on blessing the generations, despite humanity's consistent rebellion against him. In brief, if it is the case that the descendants of Adam and Eve continue to reap the consequences of their autonomy, God remains resolute in his desire to rescue the cosmos.

But it is when the Creator establishes a relationship with a man called Abram – whose name would be eventually modified to Abraham – that a crucial turning point occurs in the story. Genesis 12 marks the transition from the primeval stages of the world to the moment God starts to reveal himself to humanity in more particular ways. In the words of Christopher Wright, "what

---

2. It is important to note here that the commission Noah receives from God in Gen 9:1–7 is in partial continuity with the commandment given to humanity in Gen 1:28–30.

we have here in Genesis 12:1–3 is the launch of God's *redemptive* mission."[3] It is to Abraham that God unveils facets of his character and thus begins to deal with the source of the problem initiated in Genesis 3.[4]

Indeed, Abraham is so important that the opening book of the New Testament canon introduces Jesus in direct connection with the Old Testament patriarch: "An account of the genealogy of Jesus the Messiah, the son of David, the son of Abraham" (Matt 1:1). Perhaps it wouldn't be an exaggeration to say that, according to the Gospel of Matthew, the Bible should be divided into Genesis 1–11 and Genesis 12 onwards.

But what exactly happens to Abraham that becomes so paradigmatic to the rest of the biblical plot? If we pay attention to the account of his life, we will notice that what makes Abraham distinct is nothing more than God's promises to him. Of all the things that the Creator says and does throughout the patriarch's journey, none concern Abraham as an isolated individual. Yes, God repeatedly states his blessings on the patriarch, but says the blessings are meant ultimately for "all the families of the earth" to be blessed. That is to say, the benefits Abraham would receive from his relationship with God were not ends in themselves, but the very means to the revelation of the divine wisdom to the ends of the world.

It is by no means irrelevant in this regard that implicit to God's sovereign choice of Abraham is the fact that the latter had absolutely no merit to boast of in the realization of the divine purposes: in addition to Abraham himself being advanced in age, his wife Sarah was barren. Nevertheless, a "great nation" would be formed from the descendant God was about to give them. In the light of this, to question why God chose Abraham instead of another person, as many Christians do, is to ask the wrong sort of question, since the call of Abraham had to do primarily with God's faithfulness to his word.

One would need an entire book to treat all the details of the story of Abraham, but suffice it to underscore that God promises him and Sarah an "offspring" – in Hebrew, *zera ʿ* – through whom the nations could perceive God's goodness. Besides the impossibility of that happening apart from divine intervention, we must note that the term "offspring" hearkens back to what the Creator had said to the serpent at the moment Adam and Eve were expelled from Eden: "I will put enmity between you and the woman, and between

---

3. C. J. H. Wright, *Seven Sentences*, 43 (emphasis original).

4. Of course, we do occasionally encounter God-fearing people in Gen 4–11, such as Abel and Noah. But the clear perception of God's glory has become a distant memory after Gen 3. The best people could do until Gen 12, when Abraham was still called Abram, was to "grope" for the divine attributes (cf. Acts 17:27).

your offspring [*zera '*] and hers; he will strike your head, and you will strike his heel" (Gen 3:15). In its original context, the utterance in Genesis 3 pointed forward to the perennial conflict which would characterize human existence in a world wherein chaos and death had become inescapable facts. Nevertheless, by making this specific promise to Abraham, God anticipates the hope that such a conflict would one day be resolved: the "offspring" of the patriarch – and, by implication, of "the woman" – would prevail over the effects of sin. In the generations of Abraham's future descendants, all the nations of the earth would see the glory of God.

Most instructive still, however, is the fact that the divine plan would never have been fulfilled if it depended on Abraham's ethical integrity or confidence in what God had said. His limitations are well known: he falls short of showing exemplary courage both in Egypt and in Gerar (cf. Gen 12:10–20; 20:1–18), and his attempt at "helping" God by following Sarah's idea to get a child with Hagar does not end terribly well (cf. Gen 16:1–16). It is thus somewhat comforting, at least for me, to know that someone as flawed as Abraham came to be known as "the father of faith." It would surely be more appropriate to call him "the son of God's faithfulness."

But this is precisely the force of his story. About twenty years after they were summoned out of the land of his ancestors, and in spite of the remarkable inconsistencies in their characters, Abraham and Sarah do become parents to Isaac:

> The LORD dealt with Sarah as he had said, and the LORD did for Sarah as he had promised. Sarah conceived and bore Abraham a son in his old age, at the time of which God had spoken to him. Abraham gave the name Isaac to his son whom Sarah bore him. (Gen 21:1–3)

And, when Abraham and Sarah hold Isaac in their arms, they finally realize that God is utterly faithful. So much so that, a few years later, Abraham does not hesitate to offer his beloved son to God in Moriah (cf. Gen 22:1–19). Many centuries later, the author of the book of Hebrews would interpret this last event in terms of the patriarch's confidence in the God who keeps his promises: "By faith Abraham, when put to the test, offered up Isaac. He who had received the promises was ready to offer up his only son. . . . He considered the fact that God is able even to raise someone from the dead – and figuratively speaking, he did receive him back" (Heb 11:17, 19).

Beginning in Genesis 12, therefore, the Creator initiates his redemptive plan, opening up – even if partially – an alternative way of life, one contrary to human autonomy. He does that by demonstrating his faithfulness, despite all the inauspicious circumstances of Abraham's life. Among the many things that Abraham was taught after his departure from Ur of the Chaldeans, the most fundamental lesson was this: God is absolutely trustworthy. This is crucial, for since the garden of Eden the basis of humanity's fellowship with the Creator – on which the cosmos itself could have been maintained as a cosmic temple – has always been trust. It does not come as a surprise to see that Paul explains the centrality of faith in Jesus Christ by mentioning the very example of Abraham: the patriarch "believed God, and it was reckoned to him as righteousness" (Rom 4:3; cf. Gen 15:6).[5]

But Abraham is not the end of the story. There is much more that God has to teach about himself to humanity, and there is even more to be fixed, if the universe is to be definitively restored. However, before we turn to the next chapter, I must make one last observation. The same God who appeared to Abraham still wants to be known by each one of us today. He hasn't changed, as he never does. In fact, every single person who has come to believe in the God presented in the Scriptures is part of the "all the families of the earth" which would be blessed through the descendants of Abraham. And it is precisely because our stories are connected to the story of Abraham that we need to be reminded that God calls us to learn the very same lesson the patriarch had to learn. (We are actually in a more advantageous position than Abraham, since we can look back to Genesis and see all the pieces of the biblical puzzle already put together.) It is not reasonable, then, to expect that our journeys will be filled with certainty and comfort all the time. Life's incongruities are intrinsic to the post-fall world which we ourselves continue to build; dealing with them is a key element in God's pedagogical process of restoring his image in us.

More to the point, trust in God is the most elementary aspect of human vocation, essential for the redemption of the cosmos to begin to happen. The story of Abraham is good news indeed. In it, we see that God is committed both to rescuing his creation and to fulfilling his purposes for humanity. Likewise, our stories too are the stage on which his faithfulness manifests itself. Our journeys are all about his insistence on reconciling to himself our lives and his world.

---

5. Paul seems to disagree with the author of Sirach 44:19–21, who claims: "Abraham was the great father of a multitude of nations, and no one has been found like him in glory. He kept the law of the Most High, and entered into a covenant with him; he certified the covenant in his flesh, and when he was tested he proved faithful. Therefore the Lord assured him with an oath that the nations would be blessed through his offspring; that he would make him as numerous as the dust of the earth, and exalt his offspring like the stars, and give them an inheritance from sea to sea and from the Euphrates to the ends of the earth."

4

Free for a New Start: The Exodus as the Beginning of New Creation

As Pharaoh drew near, the Israelites looked back, and there were the Egyptians advancing on them. In great fear the Israelites cried out to the LORD. They said to Moses, "Was it because there were no graves in Egypt that you have taken us away to die in the wilderness? What have you done to us, bringing us out of Egypt? Is this not the very thing we told you in Egypt, 'Let us alone and let us serve the Egyptians'? For it would have been better for us to serve the Egyptians than to die in the wilderness." But Moses said to the people, "Do not be afraid, stand firm, and see the deliverance that the LORD will accomplish for you today; for the Egyptians whom you see today you shall never see again. The LORD will fight for you, and you have only to keep still." (Exod 14:10–14)

I was recently told by one of my church members, who unlike me is very active on social media, that every now and then Rev. Timothy Keller says on Twitter, "Christians need the gospel as much as non-Christians do." Yes, absolutely, and the only thing I would add is this: we don't have to wait for the biblical plot to reach the New Testament to realize the veracity of this statement. Already in Genesis, the most fundamental reality that separates the "good guys" from the "villains" is the work of God's grace on them. We like to use the epithet "heroes of faith" to refer to our favorite biblical characters, but ultimately such a description seems too optimistic regarding the human condition. So far in the Bible, there have been no perfect "heroes," in the plural. God is the only protagonist of the narrative.

As we continue to read the rest of Genesis, we notice that what has begun in Abraham does continue to unfold in the lives of his son Isaac, his grandson Jacob, and his many great-grandchildren. And yet, if we compare the story of Abraham's descendants from Genesis 23 onwards with the episodes prior to Genesis 12, it is difficult to see any significant difference between them with regards to people's moral integrity. Isaac repeats some of the mistakes of his father (cf. Gen 26:1–25). The relationship between Esau and Jacob is fraught with intrigue, family division, and betrayal (cf. 25:27–35; 27:1–46). And, in the third generation, we witness a reprise of sorts, not of Noah's obedience, but of Cain's crime against Abel: Joseph is sold as a slave by his own brothers (cf. 37:12–36). Clearly, in spite of the divine promises to bless all the nations through Abraham's family, humanity has remained the same since the fall.

Consequently, the emphasis given in Genesis 3–11 finds a loud echo in Genesis 12–50: that is, if there is hope, it is only because God takes the leading role and stays loyal to his own purposes. There are no heroes besides. Human merit – our ability to reverse chaos and death, restoring heaven and earth as God's sacred space – simply doesn't exist after Genesis 3. This is why the first book of the Bible concludes by pointing us forward to the continuation of God's gracious intervention in human history. Indeed, after several plot twists and U-turns, Joseph, who by then had become minister to the most powerful ruler of that time, discerns how God's redemptive purposes should inform his response to the injustices he had suffered from his brothers: "Even though you intended to do harm to me, God intended it for good, in order to preserve a numerous people, as he is doing today. So have no fear; I myself will provide for you and your little ones" (Gen 50:20–21). As a result, Abraham's descendants – now referred to in the biblical pages as "the Hebrews" – end up enjoying great prosperity in the most robust economy of that time: Egypt.

Nevertheless, in a post-fall world, wealth is transient. The cosmos as a whole still aches with the brokenness caused by sin, and so there is no unconditionally guaranteed security outside the garden of Eden. And it is at this point that the Bible introduces us to another major character, one who will play a significant role in the plot of salvation.

Moses enters the stage roughly four centuries after the settlement of Joseph's family in Egypt, in a context in which their good fortune had already waned. In fact, a change of pharaonic dynasties had placed the descendants of Abraham under severe oppression: "Now a new king arose over Egypt, who did not know Joseph. He said to his people . . . 'Come, let us deal shrewdly with them'" (Exod 1:8–10). Intriguingly, though, the text says nothing about the Hebrews actively asking for God's aid. Could it be that centuries of pursuit of the "Egyptian way of life" ended up occasioning some degree of amnesia concerning the one who had called their forefathers to be a blessing to all the nations? In any case, before Abraham's descendants even cry out to God, God himself takes the initiative to approach them – who are no longer merely a family, as they have become a numerous people. In resemblance to what had happened to Noah, then, Moses is taken out of the waters (cf. Exod 2:5–6), and later on God reveals himself to him (3:4).

The prominence of Moses is evident in the fact that he is the leader chosen by God to deliver the Hebrews from the bondage of Egypt. The exodus, however, is much more than the miraculous liberation of a people crushed by a wicked empire: it is also the carrying on of that which had been started in Abraham. In the famous encounter at the burning bush, God does not identify himself as a generic force, but rather as the one who had given his promises to the patriarchs: "I am the God of your father, the God of Abraham, the God of Isaac, and the God of Jacob" (Exod 3:6). The exodus is important, therefore, because it leads to the formation of "a great nation" with a proper name, in continuity with what had been announced to Abraham – that his descendants would finally become Israel. (We will talk specifically about Israel in the next chapter.)

At this point, it is highly relevant that the word "salvation" (*yešuʿāh*) – so pivotal to us Christians, and so consequential for our understanding of the biblical message – occurs in deep connection with the event of the Hebrews' departure from Egypt (cf. Exod 14:13). Prior to this, the term is used in Genesis 49:18, in Jacob's prophecies regarding the future of his children. This indicates that whatever we make of "salvation" as a theological concept, it must be properly anchored in what God originally revealed when Abraham's descendants left the land of Pharaoh. In chapter 11, we will see that the gospels articulate the saving work of Jesus by using imagery borrowed straight from the second book of the Bible.

We need therefore to ask, in what terms does God accomplish his "salvation" in the exodus? The overall story of Moses's early years is well known. Having been preserved from death while still a baby, he is raised by his own mother at the court of Pharaoh (Exod 2:1–10). As a young adult, he has to flee to the region of the Midianites after killing an Egyptian worker, and eventually marries Zipporah, thus also becoming the shepherd to his father-in-law's flock (2:11–22). And it is when Moses is looking after Jethro's animals in the desert that God commissions him as well as reveals his personal name for the first time: "I AM WHO I AM" – YHWH (3:14–15).

The fact that this encounter happens in the wilderness is by no means insignificant. In the Bible, the desert often functions as a symbol of desolation. That place, however, where YHWH manifests his presence to Moses at the burning bush temporarily becomes a sacred space and hence is called "holy ground" (Exod 3:5). This sets the scene for the climax of the exodus – namely, when the glory of YHWH finally descends to dwell among the Israelites at the tabernacle (cf. Exod 38) – which in many ways reverses the event of Genesis 3, when Adam and Eve were denied access to the garden of Eden.

From a perspective that considers the theological unity of the Pentateuch, moreover, it is significant that the supreme leader of Egypt wore a snake-shaped crown. The biblical text is not concerned about giving us this historical detail, but the earliest readers would have likely known that Pharaoh was seen in identification with the Egyptian serpent-god.[1] Given that the serpent was conspicuous in the fall, Exodus seems to depict Pharaoh as aligning himself with the forces of chaos in his abuse of the descendants of Abraham – who, since Genesis 1–2, were all bearers of the image of the Creator. This is what seems to be implicit in God's referring to Israel as his "firstborn son," when he instructs Moses to return to Egypt to carry out the divine plan: "'Thus says the LORD: Israel is my firstborn son. I said to you [Pharaoh], "Let my son go that he may worship me." But you refused to let him go; now I will kill your firstborn son'" (Exod 4:22–23). If the reader has been attentive to the sequence of the biblical plot so far, it is difficult not to see the exodus as representing the conflict between the descendants of Abraham (and also of Eve) and the realities symbolized by the serpent in Genesis 3 and now lived out by Pharaoh. Through Israel – Abraham's descendants and YHWH's "firstborn son" – chaos would be faced.

In the light of this, it becomes clear what is really at stake when the Hebrews leave the land of Egypt: YHWH's faithfulness to his promises results in a head-on confrontation with the tyranny perpetrated by Pharaoh. This is why the most momentous events in the exodus are the ten plagues and the crossing of the Red Sea.

As with the seven-day creation account, the ten plagues were theologically rich for ancient readers. Each of the plagues represents YHWH's judgment on the Egyptian gods, who were seen as responsible for sustaining the order of the cosmos, including Pharaoh's firstborn. YHWH's interventions culminating

---

1. Walton, Matthews, Chavalas, *Old Testament*, 80, 82.

in the exodus, therefore, demonstrate that said entities are simply parodies of the order that God had established in the beginning: "I will pass through the land of Egypt that night, and I will strike down every firstborn in the land of Egypt, both human beings and animals; on all the gods of Egypt I will execute judgments: I am the LORD" (Exod 12:12).

Indeed, YHWH's self-identification as "I AM WHO I AM" probably develops the same theme. In antiquity, names connoted the specific functions of the gods in the visible realm of nature.[2] When Moses asks for the divine name in Exodus 3:13, he wants to know how God fits within the rest of the Egyptian pantheon. YHWH, by contrast, can never be reduced to such categories, for he is the very source of all existence, the one who is absolutely free to define himself: "Thus you shall say to the Israelites, 'I AM has sent me to you'" (3:14). By pouring out his judgment on Egypt, then, God dismantles their cosmology – and, consequently, their worldview – and reveals himself as the only Creator of the cosmos. And the supreme authority of YHWH included his ability to harden Pharaoh's own stubborn heart, so that wickedness would serve to exalt the power and the goodness of Israel's God (cf. Exod 4:21; 7:3, 13–14, 22; 8:15, 19, 32; 9:7, 12, 34–35; 10:20, 27; 11:10; 14:5, 8).

In the same vein, the crossing of the Red Sea indicates the beginning of the restoration of God's order in the universe. Note the wealth of imagery in 14:15–22:

> Then the Lord said to Moses, "Why do you cry out to me? Tell the Israelites to go forward. But you lift up your staff, and stretch out your hand over the sea and divide it, that the Israelites may go into the sea on dry ground. Then I will harden the hearts of the Egyptians so that they will go in after them; and so I will gain glory for myself over Pharaoh and all his army, his chariots, and his chariot drivers. And the Egyptians shall know that I am the LORD, when I have gained glory for myself over Pharaoh, his chariots, and his chariot drivers."
>
> The angel of God who was going before the Israelite army moved and went behind them; and the pillar of cloud moved from in front of them and took its place behind them. It came between the army of Egypt and the army of Israel. And so the cloud was there with the darkness, and it lit up the night; one did not come near the other all night.

---

2. Rose, "Names of God," 1002–11.

> Then Moses stretched out his hand over the sea. The LORD
> drove the sea back by a strong east wind all night, and turned the
> sea into dry land; and the waters were divided. The Israelites went
> into the sea on dry ground, the waters forming a wall for them on
> their right and on their left.

In the same context where the term "salvation" is associated with YHWH's concrete act of liberating Abraham's descendants from slavery, the Bible also says that there is "darkness" (*ḥōšek*) on the side of the Egyptians, whereas Israel is protected with "light" (*'ôr*) (Exod 14:19–20; cf. 13:20–22). This language is reminiscent of Genesis 1–2, where the Creator separates "darkness" (*ḥōšek*) from "light" (*'ôr*) on the first day of creation. What is more, at the most critical juncture of the passage, a "wind" (*rûaḥ*) drives back the sea, to the point that the "waters" (*mayim*) were divided. The Hebrew word *rûaḥ*, translated as "wind" in Exodus 14:21, is the very same word for the "Spirit" of God that fluttered over the "waters" (*mayim*) in Genesis 1:2. And, in Exodus, the *rûaḥ* opens the Red Sea in order for the Israelites to cross to the other side on "dry ground" (*yabbāšāh*), which hearkens back to the "dry ground" (*yabbāšāh*) that appeared with the separation of the "waters" (*mayim*) in Genesis 1:9. Furthermore, the same *rûaḥ* blows from the "east" (*qādîm*), which is precisely where, according to Genesis 2:8, God had planted the garden of Eden: "And the LORD God planted a garden in Eden, in the east."[3]

The crowd who actually departed from Egypt with Moses may not have realized all these connections, but reading Exodus in continuity with Genesis helps us to see the thematic coherence within the two books. In highlighting the ten plagues and the crossing of the Red Sea in language that hearkens back to Genesis 1–2, Exodus underlines the continuity between the creation of the cosmos and the liberation of the descendants of Abraham, portraying the latter as the beginning of the reordering of the cosmos which was messed up by sin.

Much more than a series of spectacular miracles, therefore, the exodus represents the beginning of a new creation. This explains why the crossing of the Red Sea cannot culminate in any event other than the presence of God among his people at the tabernacle. In fact, as we will see shortly, the tabernacle was intended to evoke Eden.[4] The difference, of course, is that this new creation presupposes the reality broken by sin, so that the manifestation of the divine presence is restricted, at least for the time being, to a tent. But it's a start

---

3. Cf. Provan, *Seriously Dangerous Religion*, 38–40.

4. See further Beale and Kim, *Deus Mora entra Nós* [*God Dwells among Us*], 33–44.

nonetheless: God has already begun to carry out his plan to restore the cosmos as his dwelling space.

By implication, we see in the exodus that God's salvation entails judgment on every entity which foments chaos. Even today he opposes every pattern of thought that contradicts the vision presented in Genesis 1–2: God resists all kinds of "incarnations" of the serpent. The tenth plague, in particular, eloquently corroborates the statement by Mr. Beaver in C. S. Lewis's *The Lion, the Witch and the Wardrobe*: God is perfectly good, but it's a terrible idea to play around with his holiness. If Pharaoh was visited with such a terrible judgment, we should expect the same outcome upon all those who perpetrate evil in the world – even if only on the day when God's salvation will be finally consummated. And this brings us hope. When we look at the exodus, we remember that YHWH never forgets what justice is: he is utterly committed to putting all things in their right place.

More positively, though, it is important to state once again that, according to Exodus, God's salvation is about new creation. Far from a mere "feeling" that we have after repeating a prayer, salvation is the concrete expression of God's intervention in history, wherein he confronts the chaos that holds us in bondage. YHWH saves the descendants of Abraham from Egypt by disrupting every perception of reality and every value system that is not in line with his character, leading Israel into his presence. And, again, we should not be surprised if some fundamental structures of our lives are deeply shaken when we encounter the God who reveals himself through this story, so that we may live in the light of who he is. This is very good news. We may find ourselves comfortably settled in for the way of life of this world, but the exodus shows us that such an accommodation is often a subtle form of bondage. In Egypt, YHWH turns everything upside down, in order to show us that, in fact, it is the reality of Egypt that is upside down. To speak of salvation is to speak of how God frees us from the problem that originated in Genesis 3.

We need to make one last observation before moving on to the next episode. The exodus ended up distinguishing two major groups of people: those who were visited by YHWH's judgment and those who were saved by his hand. This division happened decisively in the last plague, right before the actual departure, when the angel of destruction killed all the firstborn in Egypt – the first Passover (cf. Exod 12:1–51). More importantly, the only thing that determined the difference between those destroyed and those preserved was the blood of an innocent animal, sacrificed on that same day in accordance with YHWH's command. In other words, the salvation of the Hebrews was never about some intrinsic merit they could supposedly boast of before God more than the Egyptians. It is significant that the exodus was available to foreigners as well as to the descendants of Abraham: "A mixed crowd also went up with them, and livestock in great numbers, both flocks and herds" (Exod 12:38; cf. 12:43–49). So the only thing that ensured the people's deliverance was their trust in YHWH's words – that he would keep his promise to save them from death. Trust was the point, not merit. At the center of this new creation initiated in the exodus was the blood of an animal, sacrificed to protect those who trusted YHWH's commands.

Many centuries later, someone called Jesus – whose name very appropriately means "YHWH saves" – will enter the stage, and his mission will not only begin at the waters, but will also culminate in the celebration of the Passover. Till then, however, there's still a long way for us to go.

5

Like Father, Like Son: The Calling of Israel

On the third new moon after the Israelites had gone out of the land of Egypt, on that very day, they came into the wilderness of Sinai. They had journeyed from Rephidim, entered the wilderness of Sinai, and camped in the wilderness; Israel camped there in front of the mountain. Then Moses went up to God; the LORD called to him from the mountain, saying, "Thus you shall say to the house of Jacob, and tell the Israelites: You have seen what I did to the Egyptians, and how I bore you on eagles' wings and brought you to myself. Now therefore, if you obey my voice and keep my covenant, you shall be my treasured possession out of all the peoples. Indeed, the whole earth is mine, but you shall be for me a priestly kingdom and a holy nation. These are the words that you shall speak to the Israelites." (Exod 19:1–6)

Without a shadow of a doubt, the exodus has been the most cataclysmic event thus far in the biblical narrative. The same God who had formed and filled the heavens and the earth – the supreme Creator of all things – has finally revealed himself as the Savior of Abraham's descendants: YHWH has delivered Israel, his "firstborn son" (Exod 4:22), from the tyranny of Pharaoh, the serpent-like ruler of Egypt. Through the ten plagues and the parting of the waters, God has begun to reestablish order in the cosmos, aiming at the redemption of his creation. And, at an important juncture, there was the Passover sacrifice which protected the Hebrews from the final plague – death.

But the Israelites' departure from slavery is not the end of the story. One of the main aspects of God's promises to Abraham was that his descendants would become such an influential people that, through them, all the nations of the earth would have a clear vision of the divine glory. That is to say, in calling Abraham, God made "all the families" of the planet potential objects of his redemptive deeds. This point is closely linked to the original purpose described in Genesis 1–2: as bearer of the Creator's image, humanity was called to represent his rule over the whole cosmos – a task severely compromised after Adam and Eve ate the fruit of "the knowledge of good and evil." Accordingly, the salvation of the cosmos necessarily entailed the restoration of the human vocation. In other words, the exodus would be incomplete if that crowd of slaves remained ignorant of their purpose within the divine plan for the world and without a self-perception in relation to YHWH's character.

So, when the Israelites arrive at Sinai, before building the tabernacle, where the divine presence would dwell among his people, they receive from YHWH a particular calling. No longer defined by slavery, Israel now has the opportunity to take the divine commandments as the absolute frame of reference for their entire existence. At Sinai, YHWH summons his "firstborn son" to be a nation of true worshipers. It is precisely for this reason that Exodus 19 is so crucial to the plot of salvation: just as the harmony of the cosmos hinged on Adam and Eve's dependence on the Creator, so what begins in the exodus is connected to Israel's faithfulness to the covenant with YHWH.

This means that Israel would be a "great nation," with the divine presence at its center, only insofar as "greatness" was entirely qualified by the people's reliance on the goodness and the wisdom of God. No wonder YHWH's words at Sinai are so clearly reminiscent of the role of Adam and Eve in Eden: "if you obey my voice and keep my covenant" (Exod 19:5). Indeed, this emphasis will be repeated when Israel is about to enter the promised land, at the end of their four-decade pilgrimage through the desert. In Deuteronomy 28, Moses famously exhorts the new generation of Israelites, reminding them that there are only two ways of existence: the way of obedience on the one hand, which would result in blessing and life, and the way of autonomy on the other, which would result in curse and death.

> If you will only obey the LORD your God, by diligently observing all his commandments that I am commanding you today, the LORD your God will set you high above all the nations of the earth; all these blessings shall come upon you and overtake you, if you obey the LORD your God:
>   Blessed shall you be in the city, and blessed shall you be in the field . . .

> But if you will not obey the LORD your God by diligently observing all his commandments and decrees, which I am commanding you today, then all these curses shall come upon you and overtake you:
>
> Cursed shall you be in the city, and cursed shall you be in the field . . . (Deut 28:1–3, 15–16)

In Hebrew, the expression translated "if you obey my voice" in Exodus 19:5 – more literally, "if you listen attentively to my voice" (ʾim-šāmôaʿ tišmeʿû beqōlî) – is exactly the same as the one occurring in Deuteronomy 28:1, "If you will only obey the LORD your God." It is difficult not to notice the echo of the two trees in the garden of Eden in the emphasis on the two ways in Deuteronomy.

In Exodus 19, moreover, YHWH not only recalls his recent salvific acts, but also declares that the departure from Egypt has taken place in order for him to establish a special relationship with Israel. Far from being an end in itself, this relationship should serve the ultimate goal of mediating God's holiness to the nations: "you shall be my treasured possession . . . you shall be for me a priestly kingdom and a holy nation" (Exod 19:5–6). As Carmen Imes notes, this defines the mission to express the character of YHWH, the Creator and Savior of the universe, to the rest of humanity.[1] God was not making Israel into a self-absorbed empire, similar to ancient Egypt, but rather a people through whom the human identity, lost in Genesis 3, could be rescued.

In the light of this, it is important to insist that the exodus and the Sinai covenant should not be understood apart from the climactic episode that closes the second book of the Bible. All these events culminate in the descent of the divine presence on the tabernacle: "Then the cloud covered the tent of meeting, and the glory of the LORD filled the tabernacle. Moses was not able to enter the tent of meeting because the cloud settled upon it, and the glory of the LORD filled the tabernacle" (Exod 40:34–35). Of course! The beginning of a new creation and the resumption of the human vocation through Israel must necessarily culminate with God abiding among his people, even if such a reality does not happen in its fullness just yet.

Furthermore, if we pay close attention to the instructions YHWH gives to Moses regarding the construction of the tabernacle, we will notice clear allusions to the garden of Eden.[2] The most evident of these is the curtain

---

1. See the excellent work by Imes, *Bearing God's Name*.
2. See more details in Beale and Kim, *Deus Mora entre Nós*, 33–44.

made to separate "the holy place" from "the most holy," which displayed two skillfully woven cherubim, in clear reference to the guardians of "the tree of life" in Genesis 3:24 (cf. Exod 26:31–33).

The difference, of course, is that, while Adam and Eve were appointed in the context of Eden's harmony, Israel is commissioned in the wilderness, after centuries of bondage resulting from the chaos that initiated with sin. And, while the fall became a reality when humanity still had open access to the divine presence, Israel was lifted up from an already broken condition. In order for the Israelites to fulfill their God-given calling to be a nation of worshipers and a priestly kingdom, therefore, it was essential for them to have a description both of YHWH's character and of the ethical implications of who he was. God gives them the law – Torah – as the instrument for that purpose.

Contrary to what many people still believe today, Torah was never intended to be a mechanism for Israel to become "acceptable" in the eyes of God. Israel had already been rescued from Egypt as a result of YHWH's own keeping of his promises. Even before the Hebrews cried out to the God of their ancestors, he himself chose Moses to prepare the way for the exodus. In brief, the law was not a means of accumulating merit before God. (Later, Paul will be at pains to persuade the readers of Romans that many of his contemporaries had forgotten this basic truth.) On the contrary, the law basically serves as God's disclosure of his character, granted to a people already redeemed by his grace. Torah, then, is a map of sorts, designed to assist the Israelites in their vocation to depend entirely on YHWH's wisdom, reflect his character to the nations, and preserve the sacred space where the divine presence would manifest itself on earth. Christopher Wright is on point:

> If we ask, then, whether the law was given specifically to Israel with unique relevance to them in their covenant relationship to the LORD, or whether it was meant also to apply to the rest of the nations (including eventually ourselves), the answer is "Both." But this needs immediate qualification. The law was not explicitly and consciously applied to the nations (as Ps. 147:19–20 says, God had not given it to other nations as he had done to Israel). But that does not mean that Israel's law was irrelevant to them. Rather, the law was given to Israel to enable Israel to live as a model, as a light to the nations. The anticipated result of this plan was that, in the prophetic vision, the law would "go forth" to the nations, or they would "come up" to learn it. The nations were "waiting" for that

law and justice of the LORD, which was presently bound up with Israel (Is. 42:4). Israel was to be "light for the nations."[3]

It is unsurprising that the law begins with the Ten Commandments – they summarize what it means to be a "kingdom of priests," giving specific instructions regarding the people's appropriate attitudes toward God and their neighbor:

Then God spoke all these words:

I am the LORD your God, who brought you out of the land of Egypt, out of the house of slavery; you shall have no other gods before me.

You shall not make for yourself an idol, whether in the form of anything that is in heaven above, or that is on the earth beneath, or that is in the water under the earth. You shall not bow down to them or worship them; for I the LORD your God am a jealous God, punishing children for the iniquity of parents, to the third and the fourth generation of those who reject me, but showing steadfast love to the thousandth generation of those who love me and keep my commandments.

You shall not make wrongful use of the name of the LORD your God, for the LORD will not acquit anyone who misuses his name.

Remember the sabbath day, and keep it holy. Six days you shall labor and do all your work. But the seventh day is a sabbath to the LORD your God; you shall not do any work – you, your son or your daughter, your male or female slave, your livestock, or the alien resident in your towns. For in six days the LORD made heaven and earth, the sea, and all that is in them, but rested the seventh day; therefore the LORD blessed the sabbath day and consecrated it.

Honor your father and your mother, so that your days may be long in the land that the LORD your God is giving you.

You shall not murder.

You shall not commit adultery.

You shall not steal.

You shall not bear false witness against your neighbor.

---

3. C. J. H. Wright, *Old Testament Ethics*, 64.

> You shall not covet your neighbor's house; you shall not covet your neighbor's wife, or male or female slave, or ox, or donkey, or anything that belongs to your neighbor. (Exod 20:1–17)

For the same reason, the rest of the Pentateuch almost in its entirety expands these commandments, setting out rules, first, on how to administer worship at the tabernacle and, second, on how to deal with practical situations within the covenant community. Torah is all about living in the light of YHWH's self-disclosure in the context of the exodus.

Let me mention two well-known examples. In the long section Leviticus 12:1 – 15:33, Torah is meticulous in pointing out what could make someone ceremonially impure. The point is not that the situations described in the passage – for instance, skin disease and bodily discharge – were sinful in and of themselves, but rather that they were associated with the reality of chaos and death.[4] Hence, since YHWH is the most holy God, no one in those circumstances should be allowed to approach the divine presence. Nobody would look at the sun directly, with no filter, or handle a nuclear reactor while ignoring all the safety protocols. The presence of YHWH is the ultimate gift to his people, but coming close to him in a careless manner is infinitely more dangerous. So, on this particular point, Torah was meant to help Israel minister God's glory responsibly, in a world which still suffered the effects of the fall. In Deuteronomy 22:8, in turn, there is an injunction for the Israelites to build parapets on the roofs of their houses. Since God cares about the preservation of life, it was imperative that no one should neglect this everyday safety item. Accordingly, it is clear that the law is yet another expression of the Creator's goodness, as it provides a clear pattern for the Israelites to discern his ways.

But how can we consider as a gift a set of rules that sounds more like a series of prohibitions? Does Torah not differ from the commands given to Adam and Eve in Eden, especially in its predominantly negative emphasis? We must not forget that Adam and Eve were commissioned before sin entered the world. After the fall, however, "negative" commandments are simply inevitable and actually reflect God's desire to protect his people. A few centuries later, Jesus will enter the stage, and his teachings will represent the fulfillment of the law (cf. Matt 5:17–20). At one point, he will say that the reality of God's character, to which Torah was meant to point, becomes fully visible in his

---

4. See Milgrom, *Leviticus*, and Thiessen, *Jesus and the Forces of Death*, especially the first chapter, "Mapping Jesus's World" (Kindle loc. 355–660).

own life. In Jesus, then, the divine commandment will again receive a positive emphasis: "Be perfect, therefore, as your heavenly Father is perfect" (Matt 5:48).

In sum, when we locate the vocation of Israel in the broader story that began in Genesis 1–2, we realize that what makes sense of the Sinai covenant is the Creator's decision to reconcile with himself all things in heaven and on earth (cf. Eph 1:10). And the fact that such a covenant is in continuity with the "salvation" of the descendants of Abraham indicates an important truth: to be saved is to be rescued from the oppression of sin, in order to walk freely in the presence of God, as a priestly kingdom. Just as it is important to remember that the Israelites were rescued from one gloomy condition, so it is imperative always to bear in mind that they were saved to another, much brighter future: from being the slaves of Pharaoh to worshiping YHWH. Fundamental to God's plan to redeem the cosmos is the formation of a people who will reflect the character of YHWH to the nations.

And we, the disciples of Jesus, are the continuation of this. The details of how this turns out to be the case will be explored later in this book. Suffice it to note here that, according to the New Testament, our own vocation as the people of God is defined along the same lines as Israel's in Exodus 19. Thus says the apostle Peter about those who trust in the crucified Messiah: "you are a chosen race, a royal priesthood, a holy nation, God's own people, in order that you may proclaim the mighty acts of him who called you out of darkness into his marvelous light" (1 Pet 2:9). The word "church," in fact, comes from *ekklēsia*, which is used in the old Greek version of the Hebrew Bible to translate the term *qāhāl*, often used with reference to the people of Israel gathered together.

Given that it is in Exodus 19 that we find our own defining narrative as a people, therefore, let us take heed of Peter's exhortation to his contemporaries, who, like the Israelites many centuries prior to them, were surrounded by conflicting patterns of life: "Conduct yourselves honorably among the nations,[5] so that, though they malign you as evildoers, they may see your honorable deeds and glorify God when he comes to judge" (1 Pet 2:12). Or, in the words of Jesus himself, who came to fulfill the law and the prophets: "You are the light of the world. . . . In the same way, let your light shine before others, so that they may see your good works and give glory to your Father in heaven" (Matt 5:14, 16).

---

5. The NRSV translates the Greek term *ethnesin* as "Gentiles," which I have replaced here with "nations."

Part II

From Sinai to the Exile

6

Chaos in the Heart:
The Golden Calf Incident

When the people saw that Moses delayed to come down from the mountain, the people gathered around Aaron, and said to him, "Come, make gods for us, who shall go before us; as for this Moses, the man who brought us up out of the land of Egypt, we do not know what has become of him." Aaron said to them, "Take off the gold rings that are on the ears of your wives, your sons, and your daughters, and bring them to me." So all the people took off the gold rings from their ears, and brought them to Aaron. He took the gold from them, formed it in a mold, and cast an image of a calf; and they said, "These are your gods, O Israel, who brought you up out of the land of Egypt!" When Aaron saw this, he built an altar before it; and Aaron made proclamation and said, "Tomorrow shall be a festival to the LORD." They rose early the next day, and offered burnt offerings and brought sacrifices of well-being; and the people sat down to eat and drink, and rose up to revel. (Exod 32:1–6)

When I was about to prepare the outline of this chapter, I encountered a story told by Brazilian journalist Josmar Jozino which provoked in me a good deal of reflection. It was about a man called Lupércio Ferreira de Lima, a former masseur of professional athletes who ended up sentenced to prison for drug trafficking in the 1950s:

Convicted for trafficking, Lupércio spent half of his lifetime in prison. By the 1950s, he had already become a guest at the now defunct Tiradentes prison, during the time when prisoners still wore black-and-white striped uniforms. Throughout those years, he got to live with a number of famous criminals (such as the Red-Light Bandit Meneguetti, Promessinha, among others). Considered "the oldest detainee in Brazil," Lupércio became much loved in Carandiru prison, where he was granted access to all the different pavilions. His cell was sometimes open for 24 hours a day. A former masseur to the Basketball National Team and to São Paulo Football Club, Lupércio watched eleven World Cups in jail, from 1958 to 1998.

In July 1998, Lupércio was finally released. Having nowhere to go, however, he did not want to stay away from jail. He even declined the help of some friends, who insisted on paying for a long-term stay on Avenida Duque de Caxias. Instead, every night, Lupércio would go back to prison, to spend the night in a cubicle used for the inspection of visitors. And the prison officers themselves would bring him breakfast, lunch, and dinner on a daily basis. These same officers told me once that Lupércio had been given a temporary release permit already in the 1980s. But, as soon as he arrived at Praça da República, he got a portion of marijuana and anonymously called the police, reporting that there was a black man selling drugs at that place. The black man was Lupércio himself. He was immediately taken back to the detention center. That was when he received the nickname Mala. . . .

Free, Lupércio continued to sleep in prison until his passing in 2001.[1]

I am not in a position to draw any conclusions about the real reasons for Lupércio's decision, but his story got me thinking: How many times have I acted like him, even if for very different reasons and in different circumstances? Perhaps we can all relate to this. Is it not the case that, once we get used to the environment we are in, we see danger outside our comfort zone? The problem is that if the space we are accustomed to is a cell, freedom itself can be perceived as an even more terrible form of prison.

The book of Exodus tells us how Abraham's descendants were delivered from the oppression of chaos and established as a "kingdom of priests" at Sinai, called to mediate the divine presence to all the nations. YHWH accomplishes these things by indicating the beginning of a new creation and appointing

---

1. Jozino, *Cobras e Lagartos*, 77 (my translation).

Israel as the people who would resume the human vocation abandoned by Adam and Eve in Genesis 3. It is no coincidence that the exodus and the giving of the covenant culminate with the divine glory filling the tabernacle. In this context, God also gives his Torah, whose function is to serve as a parameter so that Israel can discern the wisdom of God and live accordingly.

But did the Israelites really "listen attentively" to YHWH's voice? How soon could the nations see his glory? After forty years wandering through the desert, Israel would indeed conquer Canaan under the leadership of Joshua, Moses's successor. To a significant extent, the conquest represents the fulfillment of another aspect of God's promise to Abraham – namely, to give the land to his descendants (cf. Gen 13:14–17). It would not take long, however, before the Israelites resembled the pagan nations surrounding them, instead of faithfully keeping Torah. It is shocking, in fact, to see that, as soon as Joshua dies, things go south very quickly. We will discuss this particular part of the biblical story in the next chapter, but it is appropriate to ask at this point how the Israelites could so promptly distance themselves from their calling.

We have been purposefully highlighting that salvation is initiated entirely by God. He is the one who, by his own choice, decides to restore his very good creation. Nevertheless, we must not forget that the completion of God's redemptive plan involves the restoration of humanity. The problem is that the only thing human beings have been able to prove so far is their inability to regenerate themselves. If it is true that YHWH reveals himself as the savior of Israel, then the exodus also betrays the fact that his saving act must confront the forces of chaos that entered not only the cosmos but, deeper still, the human heart.

So, along with the mission to be a "kingdom of priests," the covenant indirectly invites the Israelites to recognize how profoundly chaos formerly affected their lives. Inasmuch as Torah points to the character of God, it also illuminates the depths to which sin has penetrated the people's mentality. It is almost as though the law showed them the right direction, while simultaneously reminding them how far they were from their goal when YHWH rescued them by his grace. (Paul seems to be alluding to a similar understanding of the law in Rom 7:7: "if it had not been for the law, I would not have known sin.") God's self-disclosure in history, in other words, reveals our own condition. Knowing YHWH inevitably leads to the realization of how fundamental the consequences of autonomy were for God's image in humanity.

In other words, taking the descendants of Abraham out of the realm of chaos could only be the start. From that point on, it was necessary to take chaos out of the hearts of the Israelites. The people, however, seem to have taken a long time to realize this. They were so used to captivity that freedom with God looked unsafe. When still in Egypt, they made abundantly clear that they would rather remain as Pharaoh's slaves. It is disturbing to see the Hebrews repeatedly plead with Moses to leave them alone, when God's emissary had already started to carry out the divine rescue (cf. Exod 5:20–21; 14:12). And just three days after the crossing of the Red Sea, the people grumble again about water and food: "If only we had died by the hand of the LORD in the land of Egypt, when we sat by the fleshpots and ate our fill of bread; for you have brought us out into this wilderness to kill this whole assembly with hunger" (Exod 16:3). Israel had left Egypt, but had Egypt left Israel?

No other incident highlights this problem as paradigmatically as the episode with the golden calf, wherein we see another, perhaps even more urgent implication of YHWH's saving acts. Shortly after the giving of the Ten Commandments, Moses is summoned to the top of the mountain to receive instructions about the building of the tabernacle (cf. Exod 24:1, 12–13). The importance of what happens next, therefore, cannot be overstated: YHWH is about to give Moses a model for the representation of the new Eden – God's dwelling place among his people.

The people, however, had no idea how long Moses would stay in God's presence at Sinai. In Exodus 24:18, the narrator tells us in retrospect that Moses remained on the mountain "for forty days and forty nights," but not even the leader of the nation knew beforehand how long his retreat would last. And, strange as it may seem, it is precisely this uncertainty that appears to rekindle the grumbling among the crowd. Having seen Moses go up the mountain, the Israelites probably imagined that he would come back in a short while. After all, the worship of pagan deities, to which the Hebrews were likely accustomed in Egypt, was a fairly predictable process. In most cases, worshipers would take the offering to the altar, before which there would be a visible representation of the god – static, deaf, and mute. All the worshipers had to do then was to perform the rituals and return home, hoping that they managed to use the powers of said entity to their own benefit. Moses, however, takes much longer than expected to return – one day . . . two weeks . . . a month – with the result that his seeming disappearance and God's apparent silence left the Israelites perplexed: "as for this Moses, the man who brought us up out of the land of Egypt, we do not know what has become of him" (Exod 32:1).

We might read these words with some degree of sympathy if they didn't suggest a more serious problem. In Exodus 24:14, Moses had given the people a straightforward instruction: "Wait here for us, until we come to you again." When the Israelites claim not to know what had happened to Moses, therefore, they are in effect affirming either that he – and God, for that matter – had lied to them or that they are simply tired of waiting. In any case, they not only are unwilling to "listen carefully" to Moses's injunction, but worse yet take offense at YHWH's own authority. By leaving the Israelites waiting "until further notice," God indicates that he does not have the slightest obligation to respond to the crowd's idolatrous anxieties. YHWH "appears" when he wishes and "disappears" also at will: unlike the Egyptian idols, he cannot be manipulated; there is no rainmaking with him. The important detail, again, is that God's supposed "disappearance" here is far from capricious: Moses is on the mountain in order to receive all the details for the construction of the tabernacle, God's very dwelling place with his people! And the only response expected from the Israelites was trust.

But Israel was not used to the idea of a supreme God, a God who considers himself the only living God, a God who demands unreserved trust. They suddenly miss that sense of security they had when worshiping those static, deaf, and mute statues in Egypt, which were always required to "respond" to the sacrifices, offerings, and incantations. Consequently, the crowd requests of Aaron, the vice-leader of the nation, that he builds an image, a visible representation of "God," which would never "disappear" from their sight.

Aaron, for his part, was too concerned with his public image. He strikes us as the kind of figure who would be constantly worried about losing followers on social media. Aaron responds in the manner of every leader who is prompt to comply with the desires of the masses: the first high priest of Israel makes an idol in the image of the Egyptian god Apis, in accordance with the crowd's aspirations. Most shocking of all is that the Israelites call that bull-shaped statue YHWH: "When Aaron saw this, he built an altar before it; and Aaron made proclamation and said, 'Tomorrow shall be a festival to the LORD [*yhwh*]'" (Exod 32:5)!

The lack of trust in the words of YHWH, therefore, led the Israelites to break all of the first three commandments of the Decalogue, which defined the core of their vocation to be a nation of worshipers: "you shall have no other gods before me," "you shall not make for yourself an idol, whether in the form of anything that is in heaven above, or that is on the earth beneath, or that is in the water under the earth," and "you shall not make wrongful use of the name of the LORD your God" (Exod 20:3–4, 7). It is certainly instructive that Aaron, when eventually confronted by Moses, reacts just as Adam and Eve previously did in Eden, by understating his own complicity in the transgression: "you know the people, that they are bent on evil. . . . So I said to them, 'Whoever has gold, take it off'; so they gave it to me, and I threw it into the fire, and out came this calf!" (32:22, 24). According to the high priest of the nation, only the *people* and the *fire* were to blame, not himself! Clearly, the effects of Genesis 3 are still operating among the people. Israel had left Egypt, but Egypt had not left Israel.

Unsurprisingly, in response to such a terrible state of affairs, God decides to no longer dwell among the Israelites. As a consequence of the building of the golden calf, the leader of the nation now is compelled to meet YHWH outside the camp (Exod 33:7–11). Sin has complicated, yet again, the possibility of the divine presence manifesting itself in the cosmos. In response YHWH suggests an alternative: he will continue his redemptive plan with Moses's offspring (32:10), insisting that his glory cannot proceed with such a stubborn people (33:3).

It is, however, at this point, when the Israelites hit rock bottom almost immediately after the exodus, that YHWH reveals the most profound aspect of his character: not only does he relent from annihilating Israel, but he also renews the Sinai covenant with them, so that his presence could actually descend on the tabernacle (Exod 34:10–17). How could this happen?

Crucial for us in understanding how this came to be is Moses's intercession for the Israelites as soon as he learns of their idolatry:

> But Moses implored the LORD his God, and said, "O LORD, why does your wrath burn hot against your people, whom you brought out of the land of Egypt with great power and with a mighty hand? Why should the Egyptians say, 'It was with evil intent that he brought them out to kill them in the mountains, and to consume them from the face of the earth'? Turn from your fierce wrath; change your mind and do not bring disaster on your people. Remember Abraham, Isaac, and Israel, your servants, how you swore to them by your own self, saying to them, 'I will multiply your descendants like the stars of heaven, and all this land that I have promised I will give to your descendants, and they shall inherit it forever.'" And the LORD changed his mind about the disaster that he planned to bring on his people. (Exod 32:11–14)

This passage has been an important battleground in philosophical discussions, not least because it suggests the possibility that the sovereign God may "change his mind." We cannot give even an overview of this issue here, but it is important to say that, in many instances, the biblical text forces us to admit that some of our dogmatic conclusions are provisional. Nevertheless, two things are clear: it is YHWH himself who initiates the above dialogue which culminates in his own relenting, and nothing prevented him from simply going ahead and destroying the Israelites without letting Moses know of his intention. So, from a narrative point of view, it seems that YHWH takes the opportunity to teach a relevant lesson through that situation. A similar case is arguably Abraham's pleading for Sodom and Gomorrah, which leads to the deliverance of Lot and his family (Gen 18:16 – 19:29). The conversation initiated by YHWH regarding Israel's idolatry is therefore likely a pedagogical movement, intended to reveal his character more clearly to Moses.

Indeed, Moses's prayer accurately reflects what is at risk: "Why should the Egyptians say, 'It was with evil intent that he brought them out to kill them in the mountains, and to consume them from the face of the earth'?" (Exod 32:12). Simply put, if YHWH completely wipes out the Israelites, he would be perceived by the nations as someone like Pharaoh – more powerful, yes, but just as cruel and sadistic as the ruler of Egypt. The stakes, therefore, are very high indeed: the reputation of the God who had promised both to redeem the cosmos and to become known to the ends of the earth through the offspring of the patriarchs depended on his response to Moses's intercession: "Remember Abraham, Isaac, and Israel, your servants, how you swore to them by your own self, saying to them, 'I will multiply your descendants like the stars of heaven'" (32:13). By "changing his mind," therefore, YHWH presents himself as someone inclined toward mercy, not destruction. It is true that no idolatrous act can forever remain unpunished by a holy God, so those who celebrated before the golden calf did end up suffering the consequences of their sin (32:33–35). Even so, YHWH is always aiming at restoration.

It is in the light of this that we should understand why God's relenting occasions another significant prayer by Moses later in the book of Exodus. Having understood the absolute priority of knowing God's character, the leader of the nation seeks to see the very glory of YHWH: "Show me your glory, I pray" (Exod 33:18). God in turn responds by giving Moses a verbal description of himself, "for no one shall see me and live":

> The LORD descended in the cloud and stood with him there, and proclaimed the name, "The LORD." The LORD passed before him, and proclaimed:
>
> > "The LORD, the LORD,
> > a God merciful and gracious,
> > slow to anger,
> > and abounding in steadfast love and faithfulness,
> > keeping steadfast love for the thousandth generation,
> > forgiving iniquity and transgression and sin,

> yet by no means clearing the guilty,
> but visiting the iniquity of the parents
> upon the children
> and the children's children,
> to the third and the fourth generation."

And Moses quickly bowed his head toward the earth, and worshiped. (Exod 34:5–8)

This is where we discover how, despite the Israelites' stubbornness and hardness of heart, the story of salvation could continue to move forward: YHWH, the author of this story, is "merciful and gracious, slow to anger, and abounding in steadfast love and faithfulness" (34:6). The redemption of the cosmos, that is, would be possible only because the Creator of the cosmos, the God of Israel, is perfectly just – he never lets evil go without consequences – while also committed to visiting his people with his love and goodness for thousands of generations.

Many generations later, in fact, John the evangelist will speak of Jesus, whose mission was to manifest – not simply by a verbal description, but in actual flesh and blood – this very same glory of YHWH which the Old Testament leader was never able fully to contemplate: "And the Word became flesh and lived among us, and we have seen his glory, the glory as of a father's only son, full of grace and truth" (John 1:14). In Greek, the last phrase, "full of grace and truth" (*plērēs charitos kai alētheias*), is the Johannine translation of the Hebrew expression "abounding in steadfast love and faithfulness" (*rab-hesed we 'emet*) from Exodus 34:6.

In conclusion, let us remember that we are not very different from the people who came out of Egypt. John Calvin was correct to say that the human heart is an idol factory (*Institutes* I.11.8). This claim may seem strange to those who have never bowed down to a statue, but an idol is simply a projection of our autonomy from God, our own fallen will. This is why idolatry is so detestable to the Creator: it is the attempt to deify our selfish desires. And, like the Israelites at the foot of Sinai, we too have the tendency to "label" our false gods under the name of the one true God. How many different types of "Jesuses" are there, in the great religious market of Western Christianity, which are nothing other than golden calves easily manipulated by our political or financial sacrifices? But God's salvation is not only about our rescue from the chaos around us; it is our liberation from ourselves and from the abominable idols we stubbornly manufacture. To be saved does not stop with our being taken out of Egypt; it means to have the reality of Egypt taken out of us.

7

At a Snail's Pace: The Days of the Judges

Then the Israelites did what was evil in the sight of the LORD and worshiped the Baals; and they abandoned the LORD, the God of their ancestors, who had brought them out of the land of Egypt; they followed other gods, from among the gods of the peoples who were all around them, and bowed down to them; and they provoked the LORD to anger. . . .

Then the LORD raised up judges, who delivered them out of the power of those who plundered them. Yet they did not listen even to their judges; for they lusted after other gods and bowed down to them. They soon turned aside from the way in which their ancestors had walked, who had obeyed the commandments of the LORD; they did not follow their example. (Judg 2:11–12, 16–17)

One of the bright sides of going through this painful pandemic has been that I ended up acquiring some useful new skills. At the time I was writing the first draft of this message (it was mid-July 2020, the sixteenth week of lockdown in São Paulo), my family and I had a sudden structural problem in the kitchen. In the process of installing new water equipment, I discovered an issue in the plumbing which required not only my immediate attention, but also a remarkably delicate repair, something I had never ventured to do before. I live in an old building near the old city center, which means that any work of restoration, no matter how small, requires a good deal of competence. Under normal circumstances, I would have called a professional plumber to solve the issue with no further trouble. But because we were at the peak of the "first wave" of the coronavirus contagion, I thought it wiser to get my own hands dirty and fix it myself. Moreover, my children had rarely seen me handle the toolbox, so this rapidly became a matter of paternal honor.

The challenge was that, as soon as one part of the problem was mended, I would find another, related problem in the system. The whole incident felt like an unpleasant series of misfortunes, but upon reflection it's probably more accurate to see it as an instrument of sanctification, the kind of thing that happens usually to the person whose humility God regards as being in urgent need of improvement. To make a long story short, it was only after a few days, having resorted six times to delivery services until I finally found all the right pieces, that I was able to complete the work. And, at the end of this beating, a silver lining: I gained a basic knowledge of hydraulics, and learned that fixing one's house requires much more than good technique – it also takes an incredible amount of patience.

The golden calf incident, discussed in the previous chapter, suggested that the restoration of the cosmos would inevitably follow a somewhat tortuous path, even though God had revealed himself so especially to the Israelites. Their idolatry followed the same pattern evidenced by humanity in general since Genesis 3. So, from that point on, the redemption of creation could move forward only because the Creator remained faithful to his own desire to achieve this goal. The tabernacle ended up inhabited by the divine glory, and Israel eventually entered the promised land under the leadership of Joshua, solely due to YHWH's "abounding in steadfast love and faithfulness" (Exod 34:6). The salvation of the world is not something we can achieve by our own ability, but rather is about the reputation – the glory – of God.

With this in mind, we now turn to the book of Judges. While Judges is a well-known book, particularly for those who have taught in Sunday school, it also contains some of the most complicated portions of the Bible. Perhaps more than any other Bible book, Judges is read primarily as a source of moral inspiration, in particular for children. How many of us are used to including the folks presented in Judges in our list of "the great heroes" of biblical faith? There are, of course, a number of theological principles in the story which are highly applicable to our lives today, and there is no question that Christians have a lot to learn by knowing how God acted through its characters. Nevertheless, the difficulty with assuming that every single part of the biblical message is a blueprint for some kind of Christian code of conduct is that we lose sight of the heart of the plot in question.

Here is a classic case in point. Whenever I ask people which of the characters in the book of Judges they consider the most exemplary, they almost always respond "Samson." After all, Samson was the strongest and the bravest, the one who actually managed to kill the largest number of the wicked Philistines. Hence, we are taught that Samson is the paragon of leadership in Judges. Ironically, though, from the standpoint of Torah, Samson is probably the worst character in the story. Despite being a Nazirite – a person set apart by a vow to God (Judg 13:5; cf. Num 6:1–21) – he was also a treacherous liar, whose lack of self-control caused him often to obey his dysfunctional sexual appetite. In one instance, Samson willfully takes a honeycomb from a lion's corpse, thus breaking the law's prescriptions for Nazirites like him (Judg 14:8–9; cf. Num 6:6). In brief, if there is anyone in the Bible whom we do not want our children to imitate, this person is Samson!

On the other hand, if we make an effort to remember that the book of Judges is in full continuity with what has happened so far in the biblical story, we realize that it tells us, among other things, how the generations following the conquest responded to the Sinai covenant. In other words, will Israel "listen attentively to the voice of God" after settling into Canaan? And will they produce leaders like Moses and Joshua to model perseverance in their vocation to be a kingdom of priests before the nations?

An important detail about the book of Judges concerns its title. When we read the word "judges," what usually comes to mind is those figures wearing long robes who play the public role of preserving justice and adjudicating according to a country's law. But the people called "judges" in the Bible are quite different from our magistrates. The Hebrew term, *šōpᵊṭîm*, should be taken here simply to mean "leaders." So the main characters of the book in question act as tribal leaders within Israel, appointed by YHWH in the years following Moses and Joshua.

And what is the core of its story? While the historical details surrounding each episode are complex, the overall plot is relatively simple. The programmatic passage in Judges 2:10–23 gives us the narrator's theological vantage point: despite the settlement into the promised land, it was still evident that the reality of Egypt had not yet left the Israelites. The people called to bear the character of YHWH before the nations quickly resembled those around them: "they abandoned the LORD, the God of their ancestors, who had brought them out of the land of Egypt; they followed other gods, from among the gods of the peoples who were all around them, and bowed down to them; and they provoked the LORD to anger" (Judg 2:12). As a result, in accordance with what God himself had announced in Deuteronomy 28, sin repeatedly placed Israel under the oppression of the neighboring peoples. God thus responds in a way that is consistent with his justice, making it clear that the Israelites' insistence on autonomy would always result in death, just like in Genesis 3. The most essential problem presented in Judges, therefore, is the failure of pre-monarchical Israel to fulfill their calling (2:17, 19–21).

And yet, in his superabundant faithfulness to the covenant, YHWH never fails to raise leaders to deliver his people from their oppressors (Judg 2:16, 18). What is clear from the third chapter of Judges to the beginning of 1 Samuel is the constant interchange between the people's obduracy and YHWH's undeserved favor. (The story of Judges is never boring, but it is distressingly repetitive!) The Israelites' idolatry results in chaos and subjection, which leads them to cry out for divine intervention. In response, YHWH's compassion brings about liberation through a leader. The following generation forgets God's powerful deeds, refuses to live according to the law, and a new cycle is initiated all over again. "Once again, the Israelites did what was evil in the eyes of the LORD. . . . Once again, the LORD gave them up. . . . Once again, the people asked the LORD for help. . . . Once again, the LORD delivered them. . . . Once again, the Israelites did what was evil in the eyes of the LORD. . . . Once again, the LORD gave them up. . . ." And so on.[1]

At this point, the attentive reader will surely see a similarity between this repetition and the downward spiral depicted in Genesis 4–11. Just as post-Genesis 3 humanity sank into the effects of their autonomy, which culminated in the chaotic waters of the flood, the Israelites in the days of the judges followed the same path: at the end of this period, when "there was no king in Israel," a gang commits the heinous crime of raping the concubine of a Levite, an event which provokes a civil war (Judg 19:1 – 20:48). And, in the last days of the rule of Eli, the tabernacle is finally destroyed: the ark of the covenant, which represents nothing less than the presence of YHWH among the people, is taken by the Philistines (1 Sam 4:1–22).

Furthermore, Israel's condition is not the only thing that worsens over the course of the plot. More strikingly, the characters of its leaders seem to correspond exactly to the surrounding state of affairs. Commentators have noted that, from reasonably upstanding figures such as Deborah (Judg 3:7 – 5:31), the pattern steadily decays: Gideon is not only tardy to trust in YHWH, but also finishes his race committing idolatry (6:1–40; 8:24–28); Jephthah is a foolish man, prompt to embrace abominable pagan practices (11:29–40); and Samson is an immoral maniac (14:1–9; 16:4–22). If we pay close attention to these individuals, it becomes clear that, in terms of human nature, little has changed between Genesis 4–11 and the post-conquest days. Such continuity

---

1. See further discussion in C. J. H. Wright, *Seven Sentences*, 87.

gives the biblical drama an even more intense tone, since the law was given specifically to Israel after the exodus.

This is the point: God uses the "material" available to him, and the "material" available to him is "judges" who prove themselves extensions of the people's own way of being. This is why Judges is the first book of the Bible to stress the leaders' acting under the influence of the Spirit of YHWH. We often come across the statement that "the spirit of the LORD came upon" someone to enable said person to deliver the nation, and it is certainly instructive that such a phenomenon happens more often to Samson (Judg 3:10; 13:24; 14:6; 15:14). There are other reasons for this empowerment, but a key one is the need for the divine action in a context where faithfulness to the words of YHWH had almost completely disappeared.

The core of the book of Judges, therefore, is to show that, even after the beginning of a new creation in the exodus and the resumption of the human vocation at Sinai, the one "abounding in steadfast love and faithfulness" (Exod 34:6) remains the only protagonist of the plot of salvation. The restoration of the cosmos was the Creator's initiative, and this plan could be maintained only because the Creator had never given it up. For generation after generation, Israel broke their side of the bargain, but YHWH would never back down from his promises. We come to realize, then, that the redemption of the world is not merely about a one-off, isolated event wherein God reveals himself as a more powerful being than the gods of Egypt. Salvation also entails the long journey from slavery to the consummation of YHWH's redemptive plan, in which those called to live as a royal priesthood experience his constant patience and never-ending faithfulness.

We must understand the relevance of this point for us today. If God was not "abounding in steadfast love and faithfulness," the biblical story would never have found its resolution – and, worst of all, none of us would be here to talk about it. Had YHWH not responded with grace and patience to the repeated failures of his people, the Bible would probably not even exist. It is true that the moment we decide to follow in the footsteps of the Israelites in the days of the judges, we will experience the same fate as many of them: a return to the realm of chaos and, in the end, the full reality of death itself. Nonetheless, the book of Judges leaves no doubt that the human condition after Genesis 3 falls far short of making any "real" contribution to God's redemptive project. Every generation, even today, needs to learn to rely on the divine mercy and to trust in God's faithfulness.

One of the oldest heresies in the history of Christianity is a set of ideas from the second century AD which goes back to the teachings of Marcion of

Sinope. Profoundly shaped by a dualistic view of the world, wherein matter and spirit were seen as opposing realities, Marcion came to believe that the deity of the Jewish Scriptures was distinct – and inferior – to the God and Father of Jesus Christ announced by Paul. Among many other oddities, Marcionism preached that YHWH was a grim, angry entity, supposedly different from the "God of love" of the Pauline epistles. Though Marcion's ideas were readily refuted in his own day, it is unfortunate to see that many pulpits today still promote some Marcionite doctrines. A few years ago, a prominent evangelical leader in North America, who is ranked among the "most effective preachers" in the United States, claimed that Christians need to "unhinge themselves from the Old Testament."[2] Likewise, time and again, popular pastors in Brazil repeat the assertion that the God of Israel is sullen and grumpy, while Jesus came to reveal a "loving God," one whose tenderness allegedly comes with "no strings attached."[3]

We urgently need to let the biblical story inform our opinions about God. The book of Judges makes it abundantly clear that it is YHWH's love for his creation and his desire to redeem the cosmos that motivate his insistence on preserving his people. If YHWH, the God of Israel, was not "abounding in steadfast love and faithfulness," his Son, Jesus Christ, would never have entered the stage, and no one would have known the gospel. God is love way before Genesis 1:1. Jesus himself, in fact, would anchor all his teaching in Israel's Scriptures (cf. Matt 5:17–20). And this very same Jesus who taught people "to love your neighbor as yourself" – quoting Leviticus 19:18 – would constantly warn his listeners about the consequences of rejecting his words:

> And everyone who hears these words of mine and does not act on
> them will be like a foolish man who built his house on sand. The
> rain fell, and the floods came, and the winds blew and beat against
> that house, and it fell – and great was its fall! (Matt 7:26–27)

The story of Deborah, Gideon, Jephthah, and Samson teaches us, first and foremost, that God never gives up on his plan to save the cosmos, even though the Israelites are unable to achieve that. For the Creator, putting the world in its proper place is a matter of honor. The question is whether his people will depend on his faithfulness and remain in his presence. The grace of God is a necessity not only in the exodus, but in Canaan, too. And he never ceased to call the Israelites back to their fundamental vocation.

---

2. See the appropriate response in Provan, "Rightly Hitching Our Wagons."

3. A term I borrow from John Barclay. See his important work *Paul and the Power of Grace.*

Before we turn to the next episode, there is one last detail worth mentioning. As briefly discussed above, the end of the period of the judges is marked by the destruction of God's tabernacle and the taking away of the ark of the covenant by the Philistines. We thus see that Israel's failure results in the damaging of YHWH's sacred space. Due to the people's sin, the divine presence has to go into "isolation" once again. And this raises the question: how can the glory of YHWH return to his people, so that the last aspect of the promise given to Abraham may be fulfilled? How can the nations of the earth see the character of God through his kingdom of priests?

We notice, then, that the plot of salvation is somewhat like fixing my kitchen plumbing: as soon as one bit of the puzzle is solved, we discover another, deeper problem. We now realize that the story is missing a different piece: leaders who not only are seized by the ecstatic power of the Spirit of YHWH, but also model what it truly means to be a nation of worshipers. For the plan of redemption to advance, it will take a different kind of "material" – people who are so full of God's life that they faithfully live out the covenant.

8

One Nation, One Worship: The Reign of David

Now therefore thus you shall say to my servant David: Thus says the LORD of hosts: I took you from the pasture, from following the sheep to be prince over my people Israel; and I have been with you wherever you went, and have cut off all your enemies from before you; and I will make for you a great name, like the name of the great ones of the earth. And I will appoint a place for my people Israel . . . as formerly, from the time that I appointed judges over my people Israel; and I will give you rest from all your enemies. Moreover the LORD declares to you that the LORD will make you a house. When your days are fulfilled and you lie down with your ancestors, I will raise up your offspring after you, who shall come forth from your body, and I will establish his kingdom. He shall build a house for my name, and I will establish the throne of his kingdom forever. (2 Sam 7:8–10, 11–13)

We concluded our overview of the book of Judges by noting that, for God's redemptive gears to continue spinning, the Israelites would need more than sporadic acts of deliverance by the hands of charismatic figures: it would take faithful leaders who, in addition to being seized by God's power, would also "listen attentively" to the divine commandments. Therefore, in what follows as the plot transitions to 1–2 Samuel, the Bible underlines the importance of practicing the fear of YHWH even when circumstances compel individuals to do otherwise.

This is evident, for example, in the story of Ruth, whose main characters in no way resemble the great Spirit-grasped judges of that time, but nevertheless live in the light of the covenant, extending God's grace to one another. Ruth is a Moabite widowed daughter-in-law of Naomi, an Israelite who lost her husband and two sons sometime after they left for the land of Moab in a desperate attempt to avoid a famine in Israel. Unlike what the ancient reader may have expected, however, the foreigner Ruth is the one depicted as living according to the character of Israel's God, in a series of moving demonstrations of loyalty to her late husband's family. Intriguingly, YHWH never "explicitly" enters the scene in the book of Ruth, and his actions cut as less than "spectacular" in comparison to what we have seen in Judges. Even so, it is through Ruth's faithfulness that YHWH opens up the path for the advent of the monarchy: Ruth ends up marrying one of Naomi's relatives, a law-keeping Israelite named Boaz, and gives birth to Obed, father of Jesse, father of the great King David (Ruth 4:17).

It is highly relevant for our understanding of the overarching biblical plot, then, that the call of the famous prophet Samuel happens in response to Hannah's prayer – in contrast to that of Samson, for example, whose mother was, like Hannah, also barren, but never appears crying out to YHWH (cf. Judg 13:1–7) – and in the context where the boy "listens" to the divine voice in the sanctuary, where the ark of the covenant was kept (cf. 1 Sam 1:1 – 3:10). The central point is simple: through Samuel, YHWH was raising up a different pattern of leadership, one which would be based on "listening" to God and living out the fear of the Lord.

The passage about Samuel's call, wherein the boy "hears" the voice of YHWH three times (cf. 1 Sam 3:1–10), is commonly read through sentimental lenses, as though its primary implication is that "God speaks to little children." But such a reading, while popular, has nothing to do with the theological thrust of the episode. By speaking to Samuel during the rule of Eli, YHWH in effect indicates the end of the period characterized by the judges' failures – or, better, their "deafness" with regards to the terms of the covenant – which is now epitomized by the priest's own tolerance of the sins of his children (cf. 1 Sam 2:12–17). Indeed, what Samuel hears from YHWH directly concerns the impending judgment upon Eli's family:

> Then the LORD said to Samuel, "See, I am about to do something in Israel that will make both ears of anyone who hears of it tingle. On that day I will fulfill against Eli all that I have spoken concerning his house, from beginning to end. For I have told him that I am about to punish his house forever, for the iniquity that he knew, because his sons were blaspheming God, and he did

not restrain them. Therefore I swear to the house of Eli that the iniquity of Eli's house shall not be expiated by sacrifice or offering forever." (1 Sam 3:11–14)

More importantly, it is in this precise historical moment that David appears on the scene. Apart from Moses, David is the character who figures most prominently in the Hebrew Bible (cf. 1–2 Samuel; 1 Chronicles; Psalms). This is due to two simple facts. First, it is under David's rule that Israel finally obtains the status of an independent monarchy. According to the biblical texts, David is the strongest commander the people have ever seen, and his prowess is so great that he manages to bring about national emancipation from the Philistines. Second, David is the one who restores the worship of YHWH in the land. The emblematic episode of 2 Samuel 6:1–19, wherein David exuberantly expresses his joy for the bringing of the ark of the covenant into Jerusalem, represents the return of the divine glory to the center of the Israelites' identity. Surely, this stands as a high point in the biblical plot, because Israel's very raison d'être revolved around their relationship with their God (cf. Exod 19). David rightfully becomes a paradigmatic figure because, with him, not only does the nation resume its vocation, but the presence of YHWH, which had been "isolated" since the destruction of the sanctuary in Shiloh (cf. 1 Sam 4:1–11), can once again dwell among the people.

At this point we must remember that, before David's rise to the throne, the Israelites had made a request to Samuel, asking him to beseech God for a king (cf. 1 Sam 8:4–8; 10:19). At the surface level, there was nothing necessarily wrong in such a request. The law had never prohibited the people from having a monarch. In Deuteronomy 17:14–15, God had simply predicted that the Israelites would desire a king over them one day. The important detail to note, however, is that implicit in the law was the reality of YHWH himself as the ultimate King over Israel. This is another implication of the term "kingdom of priests": a nation of worshipers who serve in the presence of their one true King. So, whoever governs the Israelites, that person is to rule under the authority of YHWH, the supreme Monarch of the nation. Far from accumulating political power and turning Israel into a great empire, the role of their leaders – including their eventual kings – was thus to model faithfulness to the covenant.

Nonetheless, the Israelites' request for a king came from an unbelieving, autonomous heart. When, later on, Samuel looks back on his life, he says that the people's desire for a monarch had arisen in the context of the threats by Nahash, king of the Ammonites (1 Sam 12:12). The prospect of pagan oppression had been real since the beginning of the Israelites' settlement in Canaan, and the idea given by previous generations to Gideon – "Rule over us, you and your son and your grandson also" (Judg 8:22) – connotes that the hope for a king as the solution to the nation's problems was by no means novel. By the time Samuel was appointed judge over the nation, Nahash had gained considerable strength in the region, and the Israelites began to be anxious about the danger he posed. Hence, in addition to a deep sense of insecurity, there was also an imperial aspect to the Israelites' wish for a king. "If we have a king as the surrounding nations do, who knows – maybe we could not only protect ourselves from guys like Nahash, but also compete for hegemony in the region?" The request for a king, in itself, was not wrong in the eyes of God. Rather, the problem was the motivation: the people wanted to resemble those who defined themselves not by Torah, but by the idolatrous quest for power and influence.

Sure enough, YHWH surprises the people again by responding to their desires through a sequence of two events. In the first, God appoints a ruler according to the standards the Israelites had envisioned, and Saul is anointed king. In C. S. Lewis's novel, *The Great Divorce*, we find the insightful statement that "there are only two kinds of people in the end: those who say to God, 'Thy will be done,' and those to whom God says, in the end, 'Thy will be done.'"[1] In Saul's case, the people are allowed to get what they want. But subsequently another king, David, is established as a model of the type of leader God wants to rule over Israel. In the grand scheme of things, then, David's ascension has little to do with his own merit, but rather with God's mercy and his insistence on teaching the Israelites the way of life. In other words, his grace and determination to redeem the cosmos through his people are such that, in resemblance to the story of Joseph, YHWH brings good out of Israel's completely self-centered motivation.

One of the most conspicuous features within 1–2 Samuel is the contrast between Saul and David. We may begin with their appearance. Little is known regarding Saul on this point except that he was "a handsome young man" and "stood head and shoulders above everyone else" (1 Sam 9:2), but David surely does not have the "looks" of a king.[2] In fact, nobody cares to call him from among the flock when Samuel summons all of Jesse's sons to the anointing ceremony (cf. 1 Sam 16:1–10), and the prophet himself has to be warned by God not to consider the external attributes of the candidates, lest he miss the

---

1. Lewis, *Great Divorce*, Kindle loc. 102.
2. C. J. H. Wright, *Seven Sentences*, 89–90.

target: "Do not look on his appearance or on the height of his stature . . . ; for the LORD does not see as mortals see; they look on the outward appearance, but the LORD looks on the heart" (16:7). Furthermore, when finally forced to mention the existence of David, Jesse does not even call him by name: "There remains yet the youngest, but he is keeping the sheep" (16:11). That is to say, "Oh, the youngest, yes, but he smells like manure! What would you have to do with him?" Hence, YHWH makes it clear through this episode that he is not impressed by the order of values which attracts the attention of people affected by the reality of Genesis 3.

But it is when we compare Saul's character with David's that the second – and most significant – difference between them comes to the fore: one has a heart leaning towards God, while the other has a mind inclined towards himself. For Saul, it is more important to be a king than to serve as a worshiper – to save face is worth more than obeying God's words. For David, in contrast, it matters more to be a worshiper than a king – to trust YHWH's wisdom is worth more than amassing power and influence. One of the few things that Saul and David have in common is the empowerment by the Spirit of YHWH, in resemblance to some judges before them (cf. 1 Sam 10:10; 16:13). If we pay attention to how each of them responds at critical moments in their lives, it becomes transparent that Saul expects God to be on his side, while David seeks to be on God's side.

For example, in 1 Samuel 13, Saul finds himself surrounded by the Philistine army. But instead of waiting for Samuel's arrival, so that they might invoke the name of YHWH together, according to an order the prophet had given seven days earlier, Saul tries to appease his soldiers' angst by offering a sacrifice. The logic seems straightforward: Saul thinks he can hasten some kind of divine response through his sacrifice, an attitude not entirely unlike what we have seen in Exodus 32 (cf. 1 Sam 13:12). In 1 Samuel 15, moreover, YHWH orders Saul to annihilate all the Amalekites, but Saul thinks it is better to follow his own wisdom. He preserves "the best of the sheep and of the cattle and of the fatlings, and the lambs, and all that was valuable" (15:9), as well as the Amalekite king himself, with the excuse that these could eventually be given as an offering to YHWH (cf. 15:15). Saul thus seems to assume that he can perhaps "bribe" God into not blaming him for his disobedience. These two episodes result in Saul's rejection, because he proves himself willing "to use" God for his own benefit. Saul thinks his reign is about him, not YHWH.

In the famous battle against Goliath (cf. 1 Sam 17), in turn, David comes across as much more virtuous than Saul. In the absence of someone more capable, Saul is the one who should be facing Goliath. After all, as the leader of Israel, King Saul should confront whoever represents the threat of the pagan nations (and their gods). But instead, Saul hides in his tent, offering his own daughter as a reward to anyone brave enough to take care of the giant. Significantly, it is at this very moment that David appears in public for the first time in the narrative. He learns about the drama by chance when he brings food to his brothers in the camp by the battlefield (17:12–25). The youngest son of Jesse, the shepherd of sheep who is there simply to deliver a meal to his seven brothers, hears the blasphemies uttered by Goliath and responds as one – indeed, as the only one there – who knows the authority of his God: "Who is this uncircumcised Philistine that he should defy the armies of the living God?" (17:26). Far from being a display of courage without any sense of proportion, such a statement actually suggests a clear vision of what is at stake, namely, YHWH's honor and reputation. What is more, as the story proceeds to portray David's dialogue with Saul before the former finally kills Goliath, we see that his confidence comes from his own experience of God's saving power during the many days he has spent in the fields looking after his father's flock: "The LORD, who saved me from the paw of the lion and from the paw of the bear, will save me from the hand of this Philistine" (17:37).

In sum, Saul had many weapons at his disposal, but his kingship was not an extension of his fear of YHWH, and so he lacked the only quality needed for a leader to be victorious against the forces of chaos, symbolized at that specific moment by Goliath: trust in YHWH. Trust, however, was something that David had an abundance of. It is no surprise that, after David's defeat of Goliath, Saul is filled with jealousy and starts to persecute the son of Jesse (cf. 1 Sam 18:6–15; 19:8–11). Accordingly, the dissimilarities between Saul and David are intensified from this point onwards: the former places his personal interests above the honor of God, and hence literally goes mad; the latter refuses to take the throne by force, despite having already been anointed by Samuel, and lives as an outlaw until the death of Saul, who reigned for thirty more years (cf. 20:35 – 31:13).

David is important, therefore, because he prefigures the type of king whom Israel needs in order for God's redemptive purposes to be actualized: a true worshiper who recognizes that YHWH is the supreme ruler above all. For the same reason, it is in the story of David that the plot of salvation more explicitly links Israel's true vocation with the establishment of the Davidic dynasty, through which God's own kingdom would become tangible in the world. This is evident in some of the Davidic psalms, not least in the most famous of them, Psalm 2: "He who sits in the heavens laughs. . . . 'I have set my king on Zion, my holy hill'" (Ps 2:4, 6).

This is why 2 Samuel 7:8–17, the passage quoted in part in the epigraph of this chapter, is so relevant for our purposes. In its immediate context, David expresses his wish to build a temple for YHWH. Remember, the tabernacle had evoked the garden of Eden and functioned as a physical representation of the space where the divine presence dwelled. In the disturbing episode in which Uzzah was struck down after mishandling the ark of the covenant (2 Sam 6:1–9), David understood the importance of observing the exact instructions in the Pentateuch. (According to Exod 25, the ark must be carried by rods in rings, not by bare hands, let alone animals.) And, also in the Pentateuch, it is clear that Israel exists primarily as the sacred place where God's glory would manifest itself (cf. Exod 33:15–16). So, in David's estimation, his reign would be likely incomplete until there was a house dedicated to YHWH at the center of the nation.

In response, however, YHWH declares that it is necessary first to perpetuate the Davidic lineage. The word "offspring" (*zera'*), so significant in Genesis, occurs at a crucial turning point also in the story line of David and indicates full continuity with the divine promises to Abraham: "I will raise up your offspring after you, who shall come forth from your body, and I will establish his kingdom" (2 Sam 7:12). It will be the task of David's son, then, to rebuild God's dwelling place among his people (cf. 7:13). Simply put, the temple was certainly crucial, but the presence of the Creator could be realized only in the context where the ruler of the chosen nation followed the example of David.

Moreover, God's commitment to the house of David would be so profound that YHWH himself would be like a father to the monarch's descendant, and the monarch's descendant would be like a son to YHWH (cf. 2 Sam 7:14). The language of divine sonship immediately hearkens back to the exodus episode, wherein Israel is addressed by YHWH as "my son" (Exod 4:22). This betrays the expectation that this Davidic ruler would be the ideal representative of the people of God, the "offspring" of Abraham. And we must not miss the connection: it is in these terms that God addresses Jesus at his baptism: "You are my Son, the Beloved; with you I am well pleased" (Mark 1:11; cf. Ps 2:7).

YHWH thus makes it clear to David that the house standing for the reconciliation of heaven and earth – the temple – will be built by one of his successors. As we shall see in the next chapter, Solomon, the first Davidic heir, will indeed inaugurate the holy sanctuary in Jerusalem. But will Solomon prove himself to be the ideal descendant about whom God speaks, through whom the final redemption of creation would take place in its fullness?

As it turns out, even though his journey reminds us that we need a king who governs us according to God's own reign, David himself did not perfectly fulfill his vocation. David is not the king we so desperately need; like the judges before him, he did not end his rule well. A few chapters after God speaks about the temple through the prophet Nathan, we encounter the fateful incident wherein the king takes the wife of his trusted man Uriah, and subsequently plans Uriah's death to cover up an unwanted pregnancy (cf. 2 Sam 11:1–27). And while David does eventually repent (cf. 12:1–27), his reign from that point on is marked by the consequences of that heinous crime. David sinned, died, and remains dead.

But one thing is clear at this point: although the order of creation unraveled with the rebellion of humanity's first representatives, God's cosmic temple will be restored through a Davidic figure whose kingdom will never end. To be saved is not only to leave Egypt and to settle in the promised land; it is to have the reality of Egypt taken out of us and to submit ourselves to the King of the universe. The king we need is the descendant of David, the one for whom God has promised to set up "the throne of his kingdom forever" (2 Sam 7:13). Who is this person? Could this be Solomon? To this we now turn.

9

The (Not Too) Wise Descendant: The Fall of Solomon

That night God appeared to Solomon, and said to him, "Ask what I should give you." Solomon said to God, "You have shown great and steadfast love to my father David, and have made me succeed him as king. O LORD God, let your promise to my father David now be fulfilled, for you have made me king over a people as numerous as the dust of the earth. Give me now wisdom and knowledge to go out and come in before this people, for who can rule this great people of yours?" God answered Solomon, "Because this was in your heart, and you have not asked for possessions, wealth, honor, or the life of those who hate you, and have not even asked for long life, but have asked for wisdom and knowledge for yourself that you may rule my people over whom I have made you king, wisdom and knowledge are granted to you. I will also give you riches, possessions, and honor, such as none of the kings had who were before you, and none after you shall have the like." (2 Chr 1:7–12)

On rainy days (or anytime during the peak of a pandemic, for that matter), when it is difficult to take long strolls, my wife Roberta and I enjoy revisiting our photo album. Sometimes we invite our children to relive with us our most memorable trips, pretending that we are in those places. On one occasion recently we remembered one of our favorite leisure spots during the years I took my doctoral studies in Edinburgh: Arthur's Seat, an ancient volcano situated within Holyrood Park, near the new Scottish Parliament building and the royal family's summer palace.

Ironically, though, we never got to climb all the way to its peak. Between Arthur's Seat and Holyrood Palace, there is another mound that looks very similar to a huge rocky slope, called Salisbury Crags. Looking from the foot of those hills, one has the impression that the highest point of Salisbury Crags is halfway to the summit of Arthur's Seat. On our first attempt at a hike there, our eldest daughter Isabella was just two years old, so we thought it wiser to split the journey into two stages: we would first walk up Salisbury Crags, take a "wee" break, as they say in Scotland, and then continue our journey. As soon as we approached our pit stop, however, we realized that the top of the first hill was not midway up the second hill. There is a valley separating them! In other words, we would need to go all the way back down the other side of Salisbury Crags and then start to walk up Arthur's Seat – which, by the way, is much steeper and riskier for children than the first mound – from the ground. In the end, we were content to take some pictures and head back home, aware that every successful trip depends on minimal knowledge of the itinerary.

As we have noted in our discussion of the story of David, the plot of salvation narrows down to the figure of the king of Israel. David was the leader who, in contrast to the judges before him, gave priority to keeping the covenant and united the Israelites as an independent nation under YHWH's rule. As a result, God promised David a descendant who would be fully successful in fulfilling Israel's vocation, one through whom the redemption of the cosmos would find its culmination.

We thus turn to Solomon. One cannot speak of the plot of salvation without mentioning David's direct successor, not least given that he is the one who builds the magnificent temple in Jerusalem. We can see the importance of Solomon from the outset, for it is during his reign that the biblical story reaches its highest point thus far. After all, the construction of the temple is a momentous event not only for its physical magnitude, but most significantly because it represents God's dwelling place among his people, a reality which is thematically connected to the purpose of the cosmos in the larger context of the biblical narrative. So much so that, as with Moses's tabernacle, the most holy place in Solomon's temple is guarded by two golden cherubim, in clear allusion to Genesis 3:24 (cf. 1 Kgs 6:23–28). The consecration of the Jerusalem temple, moreover, happens in two blocks of seven days, which hearkens back to the pattern of completeness present in the creation account in Genesis 1–2 (cf. 1 Kgs 8:65).[1] It is unsurprising, then, that immediately after the inauguration of

---

1. For more details on how the Bible deploys the temple imagery, see, in addition to the works cited in the introduction, Alexander and Gathercole, *Heaven on Earth*.

the temple, two utterances connect this feat with the promises made by God to Abraham centuries earlier.

In 1 Kings 9:3–9, God restates the centrality of faithfulness to the covenant, stressing that Solomon and the people should never abandon the path of trust:

> The LORD said to him, "I have heard your prayer and your plea, which you made before me; I have consecrated this house that you have built, and put my name there forever; my eyes and my heart will be there for all time. As for you, if you will walk before me, as David your father walked, with integrity of heart and uprightness, doing according to all that I have commanded you, and keeping my statutes and my ordinances, then I will establish your royal throne over Israel forever, as I promised your father David, saying, 'There shall not fail you a successor on the throne of Israel.'
>
> "If you turn aside from following me, you or your children, and do not keep my commandments and my statutes that I have set before you, but go and serve other gods and worship them, then I will cut Israel off from the land that I have given them; and the house that I have consecrated for my name I will cast out of my sight; and Israel will become a proverb and a taunt among all peoples. This house will become a heap of ruins; everyone passing by it will be astonished, and will hiss; and they will say, 'Why has the LORD done such a thing to this land and to this house?' Then they will say, 'Because they have forsaken the LORD their God, who brought their ancestors out of the land of Egypt, and embraced other gods, worshiping them and serving them; therefore the LORD has brought this disaster upon them.'"

We must not fail to notice the connections with Genesis 2, Exodus 19, and Deuteronomy 28 in the above passage. Now that the temple is standing, it is crucial for the king to remain loyal to his calling, modeling what it means to be a kingdom of priests, leading the people in obedience to the divine commandments, and thus keeping intact YHWH's sacred space among them. As G. K. Beale points out, no other passage in 1–2 Kings has more literary parallels with Genesis 1:26–28 than the description of Solomon's greatness.[2]

In 1 Kings 10:1–13, for its part, Solomon receives the illustrious visit from the queen of Sheba, who marvels at the glory of Israel's kingdom, as exemplified in the temple, saying to Solomon:

---

2. Beale, *Teologia Bíblica*, 76.

> The report was true that I heard in my own land of your accomplishments and of your wisdom, but I did not believe the reports until I came and my own eyes had seen it. Not even half had been told me; your wisdom and prosperity far surpass the report that I had heard. Happy are your wives! Happy are these your servants, who continually attend you and hear your wisdom! Blessed be the LORD your God, who has delighted in you and set you on the throne of Israel! Because the LORD loved Israel forever, he has made you king to execute justice and righteousness. (1 Kgs 10:6–9)

Such effusive praise coming from a pagan head of state directs our attention back to what YHWH had said to the great patriarch of Genesis: "in you all the families of the earth shall be blessed" (Gen 12:3). For anyone paying attention to the sequence of the biblical plot up until this point, the prosperity of the days of Solomon – whose name is cognate with the Hebrew *šallom*, meaning "peace" or "flourishing" – has been eagerly anticipated since the beginning.

If it is true that David's first successor ushers in the highest point in the story thus far, Israel's vocation is not completely fulfilled during his lifetime. Although Solomon built the temple, and despite the queen of Sheba's recognition of the glory of YHWH, the third king of Israel falls short of seeing the consummation of God's promises to Abraham. Solomon, like his father, died – and remains dead to this day. In fact, as Solomon approaches the end of his life, it feels as if we've just heard an unfinished song, similar to Franz Schubert's eighth symphony.

Solomon's fame is also due to an episode at the beginning of his reign, the best-known version of which is in 2 Chronicles 1:7–12, where God grants the newly enthroned king a request. Of all the things Solomon could have asked for – wealth, military power, or political hegemony – he chooses what he actually needs as the leader of the chosen people: wisdom. Indeed, YHWH not only grants the king's wish, but also commends Solomon for the choice he makes. It is transparent, then, that the gift of God's wisdom would greatly aid Solomon and his kingdom (cf. 1 Kgs 3:16–28).

The important detail, however, is that Chronicles was written in a much later period, in order to encourage postexilic generations of Israelites to have hope for the future. The book recapitulates the most important moments in Israel's past, drawing attention to the qualities of the great names in the history of the people. This is why Chronicles seems much more tolerant towards the mistakes made by the kings. David's terrible affair with Bathsheba, for example, does not have the same prominence in comparison with what we are told in 2 Samuel, and Solomon's sins are likewise severely understated. The point is to underscore the positive sides of these figures, so as to exhort the reader to imitate their qualities. Another indication of this interest is the larger space that Chronicles devotes to describing the consecration of the temple (compare 2 Chr 3:1 – 7:10 with 1 Kgs 7:1 – 8:66). Again, the purpose is to look back with nostalgia to the days when the glory of God filled his sanctuary in Jerusalem, thus inspiring future generations to seek the same prosperity.

If we look at 1 Kings, however, we see a much more realistic portrait of Solomon, who despite receiving God's gift of wisdom fails to follow the divine counsel recorded in the book of Deuteronomy. Particularly instructive is the piece of information given by the narrator before the monarch's prayer for wisdom in 1 Kings 3:

> Solomon made a marriage alliance with Pharaoh king of Egypt; he took Pharaoh's daughter and brought her into the city of David, until he had finished building his own house and the house of the LORD and the wall around Jerusalem. The people were sacrificing at the high places, however, because no house had yet been built for the name of the LORD. (1 Kgs 3:1–2)

In other words, Solomon had made an alliance with the king of Egypt – the primary goal of "international" marriages was to seal political contracts – and remained lenient towards the influence of pagan practices in the worship of YHWH. The first decision represents a blatant breach of Deuteronomy 7:3–4: "Do not intermarry with them [pagans], giving your daughters to their sons or taking their daughters for your sons, for that would turn away your children from following me, to serve other gods." And the second choice betrays an explicit disregard for Deuteronomy 12:2: "You must demolish completely all the places where the nations whom you are about to dispossess served their gods, on the mountain heights, on the hills, and under every leafy tree." From very early on, that is, Solomon proved himself a man of ambiguous character: he loved YHWH and wanted to do great things in his name (cf. 1 Kgs 3:3), but had the strong tendency to relativize the terms of the covenant, achieving enviable goals according to his own definition of "good and evil." God gave Solomon wisdom, yes, but that gift should have been accompanied by fear, obedience, and trust in the Lord's commandments.

According to a commonly held view, Solomon was warped by power. David's heir is often mentioned as an example of the cliché that power corrupts, and absolute power corrupts absolutely. But upon reflection we must slightly disagree with this popular opinion. Solomon had always been tainted with the problem of human autonomy, and his heart was bent towards evil long before taking all the royal privileges in his hands. It is probably best to say instead that Solomon illustrates another maxim: power does not corrupt, but simply reveals who a person really is. It is chilling to read the somber summaries of his rule both in 1 Kings 10:21, 26–27 and in 11:1–6:

> All King Solomon's drinking vessels were of gold, and all the vessels of the House of the Forest of Lebanon were of pure gold; none were of silver – it was not considered as anything in the days of Solomon. . . .
>
> Solomon gathered together chariots and horses; he had fourteen hundred chariots and twelve thousand horses, which he stationed in the chariot cities and with the king in Jerusalem. The king made silver as common in Jerusalem as stones, and he made cedars as numerous as the sycamores of the Shephelah. (1 Kgs 10:21, 26–27)

> King Solomon loved many foreign women along with the daughter of Pharaoh: Moabite, Ammonite, Edomite, Sidonian, and Hittite women, from the nations concerning which the LORD had said to the Israelites, "You shall not enter into marriage with them, neither shall they with you; for they will surely incline your heart to follow their gods"; Solomon clung to these in love. Among his wives were seven hundred princesses and three hundred concubines; and his wives turned away his heart. For when Solomon was old, his wives turned away his heart after other gods; and his heart was not true to the LORD his God, as was the heart of his father David. For Solomon followed Astarte the goddess of the Sidonians, and Milcom the abomination of the Ammonites. So Solomon did what was evil in the sight of the LORD, and did not completely follow the LORD, as his father David had done. (1 Kgs 11:1–6)

Later on in the narrative, we discover that Solomon's opulence was enabled by hard labor and heavy taxes (cf. 1 Kgs 12:3–4); and his hundreds of wives stood for the many instances when he preferred to cut political deals with the neighboring nations, instead of having faith in YHWH for provision and protection.

So here is the explanation for Solomon's eventual failure: despite all the wisdom he had received from God, and in spite of all his wonderful achievements, Solomon did not trust the Lord wholeheartedly. What a tragedy!

The first of David's successors was endowed with divine wisdom and built the very temple of YHWH in Jerusalem, but ultimately found it safer to trust in his own ways and to break what the law had prescribed (cf. Deut 17:16–17). While Solomon is perceived at the beginning of his rule as one who "loved the LORD, walking in the statutes of his father David" (1 Kgs 3:3), he finishes his career with God's gloomy indictment: "he has forsaken me . . . and has not walked in my ways, doing what is right in my sight and keeping my statutes and my ordinances, as his father David did" (11:33).

As soon as we reach this high point in the biblical story, therefore, we realize that the problem of chaos and idolatry still holds sway in humanity, not least in the heart of David's first heir. It doesn't take even a generation from the building of the temple for the leader of the chosen people to abandon his vocation of modeling true worship. Consequently, something similar to what Adam and Eve had witnessed in Genesis 3 happens by the end of Solomon's rule: the nation suffers a profound fracture in its identity, and the kingdom is divided between Israel to the north and Judah to the south (1 Kgs 11:26–39). We have seen time and again that this is precisely what sin produces: human autonomy breaks the order of the cosmos, alienates people, and opens the path for death.

The book of Ecclesiastes, traditionally attributed to the last days of Solomon, is a great lament by someone who regrets a life not well lived. "Vanity of vanities," says the soliloquist, "all is vanity and a chasing after wind" (Eccl 1:2, 14; cf. 2:11, 17, 19, 23, 26), only to conclude that the one thing that matters is the fear of the Lord: "The end of the matter; all has been heard. Fear God, and keep his commandments" (Eccl 12:13).

Unfortunately, the long-awaited happy ending – the fulfillment of God's promises to Abraham – is yet to happen. In Solomon, at the peak of the biblical story so far, we encounter another vast, deep valley separating Israel – and, by implication, humanity in general – from the restoration of the cosmos. The ultimate son of David, announced in 2 Samuel 7:8–17, turns out not to be Solomon. We need to wait for another ruler to come.

And it is clear that the leader we depend on must be someone who does not let himself become intoxicated by the lust of vainglory. We need a monarch who, while occupying the most exalted chair in the universe, also lives perfectly in accordance with the character of God. In order for heaven and earth to be reconciled once and for all, we need a King who, from beginning to end, "did not regard equality with God as something to be exploited," but rather "emptied himself, taking the form of a slave," and "humbled himself, and became obedient to the point of death – even death on a cross" (Phil 2:6–8).

Coming from the right lineage is not enough: the true King will take the opposite path to the one trodden by Adam and Eve, by the Israelites, and by Solomon. The mountain to be climbed is much higher than we had imagined.

10

Can the Dead Come Back to Life? The Exile and the Prophets

Then the king of Assyria invaded all the land and came to Samaria; for three years he besieged it. In the ninth year of Hoshea the king of Assyria captured Samaria; he carried the Israelites away to Assyria. He placed them in Halah, on the Habor, the river of Gozan, and in the cities of the Medes. (2 Kgs 17:5–6)

In the fifth month, on the seventh day of the month – which was the nineteenth year of King Nebuchadnezzar, king of Babylon – Nebuzaradan, the captain of the bodyguard, a servant of the king of Babylon, came to Jerusalem. He burned the house of the LORD, the king's house, and all the houses of Jerusalem; every great house he burned down. All the army of the Chaldeans who were with the captain of the guard broke down the walls around Jerusalem. Nebuzaradan the captain of the guard carried into exile the rest of the people who were left in the city and the deserters who had defected to the king of Babylon – all the rest of the population. (2 Kgs 25:8–11)

According to the biblical story, all started with the creation of "the heavens and the earth" as God's cosmic dwelling place. But because of the autonomy of humanity's first representatives, chaos invaded the universe, all relationships within it were bound to brokenness, and death became an inexorable reality among those originally made in the Creator's image. Adam and Eve had to be cast out of the divine presence in the garden of Eden. God, however, moved by his irrevocable desire to restore the cosmos as his permanent temple, started to reinstall order in the world by revealing himself to Abraham and promising an offspring through whom all the families of the earth would have access to the glory of the Creator.

This promise found its partial fulfillment both in the birth of Isaac and in the momentous event of the exodus, which represented not only the salvation of Abraham's descendants from the oppression of chaos, but also the beginning of a new creation. This immediately led to YHWH's making a covenant with Israel, in the context of which the human vocation lost in Eden could be taken up once again: at Sinai, the Israelites were called to "listen attentively" to the Creator and to live as a kingdom of priests before all the peoples of the earth. Nevertheless, as soon as they received the Ten Commandments, the Israelites built a golden calf; and, even after their subsequent settlement in the land of Canaan, they insisted on following the example of the surrounding idolatrous nations. Perhaps more tragically still, the leaders of the nation also proved themselves incapable of following a different path: albeit "seized by the power of the Spirit," the judges were very much affected by the reality of Genesis 3.

Therefore God raised up David, whose story made it transparent that the redemption of the cosmos could happen only through a king who was perfectly faithful to the covenant. Indeed, YHWH promised David that one of his descendants would fulfill precisely this role. When we finally reached the high point of the biblical plot thus far, the first heir to the Davidic throne, Solomon, built the temple and received a visit from the queen of Sheba, which suggested the realization of another aspect of God's promise to Abraham – namely, that "all the families of the earth shall be blessed" (Gen 12:3). And yet, despite the great prosperity that Israel enjoyed under the reign of Solomon, David's successor did not follow a different path from Adam and Eve, and like everybody else broke YHWH's commandments prescribed in the law.

At this point, the prospect no longer seems auspicious as it did when YHWH had promised the perpetuation of David's dynasty. Israel no longer exists as a nation unified around a single place of worship, since Israel is now limited to the north, while Judah (with Jerusalem as its capital) forms the southern kingdom. This is a huge problem. If the identity of the chosen people is not centered on their worship of YHWH, there is no way for the divine promises to Abraham to be completely fulfilled. The salvation of the cosmos can never reach its culmination through a kingdom shattered by the rebellion of its kings. The sense that the Bible thus causes in us at this juncture is one of utter frustration and uncertainty: the dense, dark shadow that has haunted creation since Genesis 3 is far from dissipated. It is as though we had just received the news about the discovery of a treatment to a deadly viral disease, only to find out that the virus had undergone an important mutation, rendering the drug obsolete even before its release.

It becomes increasingly clear in the following episodes that no one is able to reverse such a state of affairs. In the remainder of 2 Kings, we see a downward spiral similar to the ones in Genesis 4–11 and in Judges. Out of the twenty rulers that the northern kingdom produces, none are genuine descendants of David – and all, without exception, are unfaithful to the covenant. In fact, the first of them, named Jeroboam, orders the building of two shrines in the north (one in Bethel and the other in Dan) and places the image of a golden calf in each one (see 1 Kgs 12:26–33):

> Then Jeroboam said to himself, "Now the kingdom may well revert to the house of David. If this people continues to go up to offer sacrifices in the house of the LORD at Jerusalem, the heart of this people will turn again to their master, King Rehoboam of Judah; they will kill me and return to King Rehoboam of Judah." So the king took counsel, and made two calves of gold. He said to the people, "You have gone up to Jerusalem long enough. Here are your gods, O Israel, who brought you up out of the land of Egypt." He set one in Bethel, and the other he put in Dan. And this thing became a sin, for the people went to worship before the one at Bethel and before the other as far as Dan. (1 Kgs 12:26–30)

To put it bluntly, though it retains the name Israel, the northern kingdom has already returned, with no shame whatsoever, to the reality of idolatry and chaos. Not even after God's giving of powerful signs by the hands of Elijah and Elisha (e.g. 1 Kgs 17:1–24; 18:20–46; 2 Kgs 4:1–44; 5:1–19; 6:1–7) do the people respond in true repentance.

The southern kingdom, for its part, manages to keep a Davidic descendant on the throne in each generation, and some of their kings are characterized by conduct which is consistent with the law – most famously, Hezekiah and Josiah (cf. 2 Kgs 18:1 – 20:21; 22:1 – 23:30). Due to the wickedness of the other rulers, however, these rulers fail to prevent the apostasy of the nation. Judah ends up permanently turning away from the divine commandments, to the point that Manasseh, the most terrible of all the kings of the south, establishes the sacrifice of children to Molech in the very temple of Jerusalem (2 Kgs 21:1–18).

How would God respond to this total bankruptcy? If we have paid attention to the underlying thread tying the biblical story together thus far – namely, the revelation of God's character and purposes through Abraham and the Sinai covenant – we know that a repetition of the end of Genesis 3 is what awaits both Israel and Judah down the road. The Pentateuch had already announced the consequences of the people's stubborn breaking of the law: "The LORD will bring you, and the king whom you set over you, to a nation that neither you nor your ancestors have known, where you shall serve other gods, of wood and stone" (Deut 28:36; cf. 28:49, 64). We must not forget that something similar had occurred, albeit in a smaller way, at the end of the period of the judges, when the ark was taken by the Philistines. Now, with the thorough failure of the kings, history repeats itself: YHWH no longer dwells among his people, and the very existence of Abraham's offspring in the land comes to an end. Just as Adam and Eve were exiled from the garden of Eden, Israel is deported to Assyria, and Judah is taken to Babylon. And this last repetition of Genesis 3 is complete: the presence of God withdraws in its entirety from among the people, chaos leaves the population desolate, and those who had been called to be a kingdom of priests return to the condition of their ancestors in Egypt – that is, as captives far from the land.

This is why elsewhere the Bible speaks of the event of the exile by deploying the language of death (e.g. Ezek 37:1–2, 11). Abraham's offspring being taken into captivity is another expression of death's entering the cosmos through the fall of Adam and Eve. The only thing that humanity in general and the Israelites in particular – as well as their kings – managed to accomplish was to imitate the autonomy of the first couple. The conviction that the biblical story gives us up to this point, then, is that nobody is capable of reversing the power of sin and death, not even the rulers of the chosen nation. (Paul will make a similar point later in Rom 5:12–21.)

So where do we go from here? If we are taken back to Genesis 3, can there really be hope? Can the redemption of the cosmos really take place?

This is where the literary prophets come into play. Unlike an often made assumption, the biblical prophets are not primarily characterized by a preoccupation with the future or with hidden, mystical secrets. While the Bible describes these figures as revealing God's specific purposes at particular moments in history, the ability to make predictions is not enough to establish whether a person is a true herald of YHWH. In Deuteronomy 13:1–18, we see that a false prophet could accomplish these things just as impressively as a genuine prophet, and in many cases what a false prophet announces can in fact take place. The Balaam episode indicates the currency of such phenomena outside Israel (cf. Num 22:1–41). The difference is that a false prophet does all these things in order to draw attention to himself or herself, not to YHWH, with the result that the people are led astray and fall into idolatry. In short, speaking of the future and carrying out great wonders are not "godly" activities in and of themselves.

What actually characterizes a true prophet is his or her loyalty to the covenant and hence to the word of YHWH. The prophet is, first and foremost, a guardian of the revelation of God's character in the Scriptures. Without exception, therefore, the biblical prophets are iconoclasts, always calling the nation to the genuine worship of the LORD. Elijah and Elisha perform powerful miracles, while Jeremiah and Malachi, for example, do not. But they all share a zeal for the glory of YHWH unveiled in the biblical story. And, since they know how God has revealed himself in the law, the prophets are able to interpret the circumstances of "today," anticipating his response "tomorrow." The prophets predict the fall of the temple and the impending reality of the exile, because they understand who YHWH is.

On this point, there is one detail which is crucial in the prophets' envisioning of the future: because they know how God has revealed himself in the covenant, they also understand that his wrath is not the final word – God's holiness and righteousness in no way contradict his mercy. In the light of the biblical story, the prophets conclude that the same YHWH who "[visits] the iniquity of the parents upon the children and the children's children" (Exod 34:7) is at the same time "a God merciful and gracious, slow to anger, and abounding in steadfast love and faithfulness" (34:6). While judgment against the breaking of the law is inevitable, the Creator's commitment to the redemption of the cosmos through his people is irrevocable. Accordingly, though they wept in the face of the calamities that would befall the nation and ended up being persecuted for their zeal for the covenant, the prophets reminded their contemporaries that YHWH would never renounce his wish to dwell in his cosmic temple.

So what exactly do the prophets announce regarding God's future plans? There are many theological emphases in the prophetic literature,[1] but five examples should suffice here to clarify this topic. We start with Amos, whose message confronts the problem of social injustice. During the reign of Jeroboam II, the northern kingdom enjoyed considerable wealth, but that came at the expense of the poor, in a flagrant rejection of the law (cf. Amos 2:6–7). At the root of the oppression of the weak by the powerful, in other words, was the problem of idolatry (cf. 4:4–5). Amos exhorts his generation to honor their true calling and to live in the light of who YHWH is: "But let justice roll down like waters, and righteousness like an ever-flowing stream" (5:24). Israel, in turn,

---

1. See Beale, 94–126.

ignores (unsurprisingly) the prophet's appeal, but the last verses of the book bring a message of hope: righteousness will visit the earth with the coming of a Davidic king:

> On that day I will raise up
>> the booth of David that is fallen,
> and repair its breaches,
>> and raise up its ruins,
>> and rebuild it as in the days of old;
> in order that they may possess the remnant of Edom
>> and all the nations who are called by my name,
>> says the LORD who does this.
> The time is surely coming, says the LORD,
>> when the one who plows shall overtake the one who reaps,
>> and the treader of grapes the one who sows the seed;
> the mountains shall drip sweet wine,
>> and all the hills shall flow with it.
> I will restore the fortunes of my people Israel,
>> and they shall rebuild the ruined cities and inhabit them;
> they shall plant vineyards and drink their wine,
>> and they shall make gardens and eat their fruit.
> I will plant them upon their land,
>> and they shall never again be plucked up
>> out of the land that I have given them,
>> says the LORD your God. (Amos 9:11–15)

Later on in the New Testament, at the Jerusalem Council, James the brother of Jesus will claim that the vision of Amos 9:11–15 finds its fulfillment in the resurrected Messiah, in whom the Gentiles can receive the "cleansing [of] their hearts by faith" (Acts 15:9).

Likewise, Jeremiah, who prophesied in the years following the reigns of Manasseh and Amon (cf. 2 Kgs 21:26; Jer 1:2), took cues from the theology of Deuteronomy and announced the restoration of the Davidic throne (Jer 33:14–22). Particularly worth noting is Jeremiah's expectation that the rule of the eschatological – that is, end-time – monarch would affect the very hearts of the people. Since the main problem of the Israelites was their inability to keep the law, the LORD promises the renewal of the covenant under the auspices of the "Branch" of David (33:15), at which point God himself would enable the nation to live according to his precepts:

The days are surely coming, says the LORD, when I will make a new covenant with the house of Israel and the house of Judah. It will not be like the covenant that I made with their ancestors when I took them by the hand to bring them out of the land of Egypt – a covenant that they broke, though I was their husband, says the LORD. But this is the covenant that I will make with the house of Israel after those days, says the LORD: I will put my law within them, and I will write it on their hearts; and I will be their God, and they shall be my people. No longer shall they teach one another, or say to each other, "Know the LORD," for they shall all know me, from the least of them to the greatest, says the LORD; for I will forgive their iniquity, and remember their sin no more. (Jer 31:31–34)

The problem is not the law, but rather the human heart, which is unable to follow the law (Paul states something similar in Rom 7:14–20). Given that the nation could never perform heart surgery on themselves, YHWH himself would do that.[2] The renewal of David's throne would involve the revitalizing of the law, culminating in the restoration of the people's lives.

The cultic and ethical implications of the restoration of the Davidic dynasty are equally presupposed by the prophet Isaiah. Despite all the calamities that were about to befall the people due to their stubborn abandonment of the covenant, Isaiah insists that YHWH would never forget the promise he had made in 2 Samuel 7:8–17. In the most famous passage where the prophet announces the coming of the ideal king, we are told that the consequences of the reestablishment of the throne will be nothing short of cosmic:

> A shoot shall come out from the stump of Jesse,
>   and a branch shall grow out of his roots.
> The spirit of the LORD shall rest on him,
>   the spirit of wisdom and understanding,
>   the spirit of counsel and might,
>   the spirit of knowledge and the fear of the LORD.
> His delight shall be in the fear of the LORD.
> He shall not judge by what his eyes see,
>   or decide by what his ears hear;
> but with righteousness he shall judge the poor,
>   and decide with equity for the meek of the earth;

---

2. I owe this analogy to my colleague Rachel Sousa.

> he shall strike the earth with the rod of his mouth,
>> and with the breath of his lips he shall kill the wicked.
> Righteousness shall be the belt around his waist,
>> and faithfulness the belt around his loins.
> The wolf shall live with the lamb,
>> the leopard shall lie down with the kid,
> the calf and the lion and the fatling together,
>> and a little child shall lead them.
> The cow and the bear shall graze,
>> their young shall lie down together;
>> and the lion shall eat straw like the ox.
> The nursing child shall play over the hole of the asp,
>> and the weaned child shall put its hand on the adder's den.
> They will not hurt or destroy
>> on all my holy mountain;
> for the earth will be full of the knowledge of the LORD
>> as the waters cover the sea.

> On that day the root of Jesse shall stand as a signal to the peoples; the nations shall inquire of him, and his dwelling shall be glorious.
>> On that day the Lord will extend his hand yet a second time to recover the remnant that is left of his people, from Assyria, from Egypt, from Pathros, from Ethiopia, from Elam, from Shinar, from Hamath, and from the coastlands of the sea. (Isa 11:1–11)

In other words, the eschatological king will rise from the ashes of the exile, be filled with God's own Spirit, reflect the divine character, and live according to the righteousness to which the law had always pointed, so that through him the ends of the earth will see the glory of YHWH. Most impressively, all these things will represent the restoration of the order lost in Eden.[3] Even though sin fragmented God's good creation, he will restore the harmony of the cosmos through the ideal descendant of David, who is also the offspring of Abraham and of Adam and Eve.[4] Indeed, towards the end of the book, we are told about "new heavens and a new earth," where life will finally flourish as it was originally intended to (Isa 65:17–23).

---

3. Cf. Beale and Kim, *Deus Mora entre Nós*, 45–55.

4. We find a similar theme in the apocalyptic vision of Daniel 7, in which pagan empires are represented by the imagery of beasts, but Israel is represented by the figure of a "son of man."

If Jeremiah suggests that the real problem resides in the human heart, Ezekiel, for his part, gives us an even more acute diagnosis. Israel in exile – and humanity in general after Genesis 3 – is comparable to an immense graveyard: "The hand of the LORD . . . set me down in the middle of a valley; it was full of bones. He led me all around them; there were very many lying in the valley, and they were very dry" (Ezek 37:1–2). In the same vision, however, God announces that, in due course, he will breathe his life over those dead bodies, so that this cemetery of dry bones will become a great nation:

> Then he said to me, "Mortal, these bones are the whole house of Israel. They say, 'Our bones are dried up, and our hope is lost; we are cut off completely.' Therefore prophesy, and say to them, Thus says the Lord GOD: I am going to open your graves, and bring you up from your graves, O my people; and I will bring you back to the land of Israel. And you shall know that I am the LORD, when I open your graves, and bring you up from your graves, O my people. I will put my spirit within you, and you shall live, and I will place you on your own soil; then you shall know that I, the LORD, have spoken and will act, says the LORD." (Ezek 37:11–14)

What we see here is the anticipation of the end of the exile – the people's long-awaited salvation – in terms of the reversal of evil from its foundation. The liberation of the chosen nation will take place through the defeat of the worst enemy of all: death will be no more, and YHWH will pour out his Spirit over his people. Needless to say, when all this happens, they will be ruled by an exemplary king: "My servant David shall be king over them; and they shall all have one shepherd. They shall follow my ordinances and be careful to observe my statutes" (Ezek 37:24). Furthermore, God's own presence will manifest itself again among the restored nation: "My dwelling place shall be with them; and I will be their God, and they shall be my people" (37:27).

Finally, we must mention the prophet Joel. Like Ezekiel, Joel also announces the outpouring of God's presence on the day of divine visitation. Joel 2:28–32, which is cited by the apostle Peter in his explanation of the descent of the Holy Spirit at Pentecost (cf. Acts 2:14–36), foreshadows the end of exile as the ushering in of YHWH's definitive reconciliation with his people:

> Then afterward
>   I will pour out my spirit on all flesh;
> your sons and your daughters shall prophesy,
>   your old men shall dream dreams,
>   and your young men shall see visions.

> Even on the male and female slaves,
> in those days, I will pour out my spirit.

I will show portents in the heavens and on the earth, blood and fire and columns of smoke. The sun shall be turned to darkness, and the moon to blood, before the great and terrible day of the LORD comes. Then everyone who calls on the name of the LORD shall be saved; for in Mount Zion and in Jerusalem there shall be those who escape, as the LORD has said, and among the survivors shall be those whom the LORD calls.

As we approach the tragic end of Israel's monarchy, therefore, we notice that there is one thing that gives us hope: the plot of redemption does not depend on us. Human capacity to maintain the cosmos as God's sacred space has always followed the pattern of Genesis 3. Yet this will not determine the destiny of the cosmos. Salvation concerns the unchanging character of the Creator – his perfect justice and never-changing grace. The only thing that keeps us hopeful as we continue to read this story is the fact that God never forsakes his purposes. If the Scriptures show death as the only thing humanity can produce by itself, they also remind us that the Author of life – who created the heavens and the earth, chose Abraham, called Israel, anointed David, and blessed Solomon – raised up messengers to make sure his people never missed this truth: that despite the exile, YHWH would not give up on restoring the world. This God never lies: David's ideal descendant will one day come and build a home for YHWH. And when that happens, it will be life from the dead.

Part III

From the Birth to the Resurrection of Jesus

11

The Coming of the Savior: The Descendant of David and of Abraham

An account of the genealogy of Jesus the Messiah, the son of David, the son of Abraham.

Abraham was the father of Isaac, and Isaac the father of Jacob, and Jacob the father of Judah and his brothers, and Judah the father of Perez and Zerah by Tamar, and Perez the father of Hezron, and Hezron the father of Aram, and Aram the father of Aminadab, and Aminadab the father of Nahshon, and Nahshon the father of Salmon, and Salmon the father of Boaz by Rahab, and Boaz the father of Obed by Ruth, and Obed the father of Jesse, and Jesse the father of King David.

And David was the father of Solomon by the wife of Uriah, and Solomon the father of Rehoboam, and Rehoboam the father of Abijah, and Abijah the father of Asaph, and Asaph the father of Jehoshaphat, and Jehoshaphat the father of Joram, and Joram the father of Uzziah, and Uzziah the father of Jotham, and Jotham the father of Ahaz, and Ahaz the father of Hezekiah, and Hezekiah the father of Manasseh, and Manasseh the father of Amos, and Amos the father of Josiah, and Josiah the father of Jechoniah and his brothers, at the time of the deportation to Babylon.

And after the deportation to Babylon: Jechoniah was the father of Salathiel, and Salathiel the father of Zerubbabel, and Zerubbabel the father of Abiud, and Abiud the father of Eliakim, and Eliakim the father of Azor, and Azor the father of Zadok, and Zadok the

father of Achim, and Achim the father of Eliud, and Eliud the
father of Eleazar, and Eleazar the father of Matthan, and Matthan
the father of Jacob, and Jacob the father of Joseph the husband of
Mary, of whom Jesus was born, who is called the Messiah.

So all the generations from Abraham to David are fourteen
generations; and from David to the deportation to Babylon,
fourteen generations; and from the deportation to Babylon to
the Messiah, fourteen generations. (Matt 1:1–17)

It was the second Advent Sunday of 2020 when I prepared the final version
of this chapter. That day, in a brilliant exposition of the angelic annunciation
in Luke 2:8–20, a member of our staff at Igreja Presbiteriana do Caminho,
Rachel Sousa, referred our community to the moving story of Darlene Etienne,
a Haitian teenager who was found alive in the debris of a school in Port-au-
Prince a fortnight after the earthquake that devastated the city in January, 2010.
The rescue workers had ended the search five days before. But as some locals
were searching what was left of their homes, they heard a voice coming from
underneath the rubble and quickly sought help. In a few moments, Darlene
was on her way to the ambulance, to the sound of a small crowd cheering
everyone involved in the girl's salvation: "The best rescue team in the world!"

I cannot recall any accounts of victims of tragedies of this sort who
managed to save themselves. It's the kind of situation where hope can exist only
if an outsider hears our cry for help and comes to our rescue. Throughout those
fifteen days, the only thing Darlene could do was to nurture that expectation.
Indeed, according to the BBC account, upon seeing the leader of the rescue
forces, the only words that came out of her lips were "thank you." If I had been
in her place, I wouldn't have had much more to say either. And that is one of
the things that Advent reminds us every year.

The plot of salvation has come to a place of frustration. In order for the
Creator's cosmic temple to be fully redeemed, human vocation must be lived
out by someone able to walk the opposite path to the one trodden by Adam
and Eve. The Israelites, however, consistently failed to fulfill the calling God
had given them: instead of resembling YHWH, they imitated the idolatrous
nations, following their own knowledge of "good and evil." Not even the
leaders of the chosen people – whether David, Solomon, or anyone among
their successors – managed to keep the covenant fully. Accordingly, God's
presence had to be isolated again, in close resemblance to Genesis 3, and the
earth's seeing Abraham's blessings had to be delayed. The exile thus serves an

important didactic purpose, which is foundational for the message of the New Testament: the repetition of Genesis 3 in the Babylonian captivity annihilates any doubts that humanity is unable to regenerate itself. To quote Paul, "we have already charged that all, both Jews and Greeks, are under the power of sin," and "all have sinned and fall short of the glory of God" (Rom 3:9, 23).

As we transition to the second "half" of the Christian Scriptures, therefore, we find ourselves at a crossroads, where the utter failure of the descendants of Adam and Eve is in deep tension with the Creator's desire to restore the world. But it is precisely because of this harrowing tone that we must also insist that the biblical story is, first and foremost, about God's commitment to his own desire to dwell permanently in the cosmos, despite humanity's insistence on thwarting this process. The one thing we can hold on to is the prophetic vision that, despite the judgment Israel deserved, YHWH will send David's heir to carry out his promises. The question is: Who can play this role?

Indeed, "tension" is a key word to describe the New Testament world. Compared with Israel in preexilic times, not much has evolved towards the resumption of the human vocation. After the years in captivity, the Israelites were roughly divided into Jews and Samaritans. Some people belonging to the former group, in particular, decided to rebuild a life in Palestine, following the edict of Cyrus of Persia. And, as early as the days of Ezra and Nehemiah, many of these Jews assumed a radical self-understanding. Having learned the hard way not to break the terms prescribed in Deuteronomy, they adopted some clearly identifiable symbols to define their identity: the temple, the study of the law, and ethnic purity (which included ceremonial concerns as well).

And yet, despite this zeal, the Palestinian Jews continued to live mostly under the dominion of other nations. After the Persians, who had succeeded the Babylonians, came the Greeks, the Ptolemies, the Seleucids, and the Romans.[1] Even following the famous Maccabean revolt, when the Jews enjoyed almost a century of independence from the Seleucids, some of their indigenous leaders were arguably worse than the ones in the book of Judges. (At least, this is the feeling one gets from reading the accounts by ancient Jewish historian Flavius Josephus, who lived between AD 37 and 100.) By the time Jesus was born, the reality of exile – and, by implication, of Genesis 3 – was still far from dissipated.[2] Just as Egypt had remained "in" Israel after the exodus, so the exile

---

1. For further discussion, see the excellent recent treatment by Goodman, *History of Judaism*.

2. I borrow this from N. T. Wright and Philip Alexander, who presented their views on the "first-century extended exile" at the British New Testament Conference in 2015.

remained a palpable experience among the Jews after their return to Palestine. So much so that the prophets Haggai, Zechariah, and Malachi had to protest against the people's complacency regarding the sanctity of the temple, and the person ruling the region in the first century is Herod, a puppet of the Romans who ordered the murder of his own wife as well as that of two of his children (cf. Josephus, *Jewish Antiquities* 15).

In the light of this, we can imagine that a godly Jew growing up listening to the biblical story, in which the Creator has yet to complete his work of redeeming the world, would navigate this tension with a deep sense of anticipation for the arrival of the one announced by the prophets. Especially during the Herodian period, many Jews referred to this figure as the Messiah (in Hebrew) or the Christ (in Greek). In other words, first-century pious Jews grappled with the messiness around them by awaiting the coming of the Messiah. Like his predecessor David, this anointed ruler would free the people from their oppressors, restore YHWH's worship, and reposition the Jews as God's "kingdom of priests" before the nations. Such a climactic moment, furthermore, would be so grand that it would represent the ultimate return from exile – or, in the language of Ezekiel, the resurrection of the dead (cf. Ezek 37).

It is in this milieu that the most important character of the plot of salvation comes onstage, the one to whom we have been pointing since the opening episode of this series: Jesus of Nazareth. As trivial as it may sound, Jesus does not come out of the blue, as if the biblical story leaped from Genesis 3 straight to the crucifixion of Jesus. And the problem with interpreting Jesus apart from the story of which he himself was a part is the risk of reducing his ministry to merely abstract ideas. Many Christians, for example, limit the significance of Jesus's mission to his death, without fully understanding how, after all, the cross was effective for our benefit. Even if we do not question the relevance of Jesus's sacrifice for our sins (cf. Rom 3:21–26; 4:25; 5:8; 8:3), this central truth should also be understood in connection with his life. If we are to comprehend who Jesus was and what he accomplished before Calvary it is imperative to locate the gospels in the long story which began in Genesis.

This is the point of Matthew 1:1–17. Matthew takes the trouble to start his narrative with the genealogy of the Messiah, because it provides the appropriate context within which to interpret the significance of Jesus's mission. We have previously noted that the biblical genealogies are more than family information, often being structured so as to make a theological point. In Genesis, for instance, a clear emphasis is placed on God's blessing of the generations, despite the fall of Adam and Eve. The opening chapter of the New Testament is no exception: in addition to presenting the lineage of Jesus, it gives us further insight into the meaning of his birth.

Matthew's genealogy locates Jesus at the pinnacle of Israel's story. Luke, too, presents an account of the origins of the Messiah, but it takes a different approach: whereas Matthew starts with Abraham and goes through David and the exile, the third gospel starts with Jesus and goes all the way back to Adam – and indeed the Creator himself (Luke 3:23–38). Matthew thus suggests that Jesus is the one fulfilling the promises that YHWH had made to Abraham and subsequently to David: through him, all the nations will see the divine glory, the kingdom of God will be actualized, and heaven and earth will finally find their redemption. To put it differently, Jesus is the one who definitively crushes the serpent's head, restoring God's order in the cosmos; he is the culmination of the long drama which began in the garden of Eden, the supreme King heralded by the prophets. (The opening phrase of Matthew, "Book of genealogy" – *Biblos geneseōs* in Greek, which the NRSV renders as "An account of the genealogy" – is exactly the same as the expression in LXX Genesis 2:4, used to introduce the account of the placing of Adam and Eve, the first couple of representatives of humanity, in Eden.)

Unlike Luke, moreover, Matthew structures the genealogy around three sets of fourteen generations: the first, from Abraham to David; the second, from David to the exile; and the third, from the exile to Jesus. In biblical literature, the number seven often alludes to the creation week, and the triple repetition of two times seven likely points to the completeness of time. As a Jew familiar with the symbolic connotations of numbers, the former tax collector Matthew presents Jesus as the climax of the plot of salvation. It may also be the case that the evangelist is using a literary device known as *gematria*, attested in the rabbinic literature, wherein the number fourteen is equivalent to the word "David." The Hebrew consonants *dālet*, *wāw*, and *dālet*, from the name of the king of Israel *Dāwid*, correspond respectively to the numbers four, six, and four, which added together make fourteen. Interestingly enough, the fourteenth person mentioned in the genealogy is in fact David.[3] The point is simple: Jesus is the quintessential Davidic descendant.

This is eloquently corroborated by the visit of the wise men from the East (Matt 2:1–12). What else would this image of important people coming from

---

3. In any case, it is important to clarify that, if Matthew in fact deploys *gematria* here, this occurrence is quite different from the so-called "kabbalistic" methods, in which supposed numerical correspondences are deciphered from the biblical text, as if the Scriptures concealed "mysterious truths." There is nothing hidden in Matt 1:1–17: the one bringing about the fulfillment of salvation is none other than the ideal successor of David.

other nations to worship YHWH remind us of, if not the queen of Sheba who, centuries earlier, had visited Solomon, David's first heir, in Jerusalem? In fact, the prophet Isaiah had envisioned the time of restoration precisely in terms of the nations gathering in Zion to contemplate the greatness of the God of Israel:

> Arise, shine; for your light has come,
>> and the glory of the LORD has risen upon you.
> For darkness shall cover the earth,
>> and thick darkness the peoples;
> but the LORD will arise upon you,
>> and his glory will appear over you.
> Nations shall come to your light,
>> and kings to the brightness of your dawn.
>
> Lift up your eyes and look around;
>> they all gather together, they come to you;
> your sons shall come from far away,
>> and your daughters shall be carried on their nurses' arms.
> Then you shall see and be radiant;
>> your heart shall thrill and rejoice,
> because the abundance of the sea shall be brought to you,
>> the wealth of the nations shall come to you.
> A multitude of camels shall cover you,
>> the young camels of Midian and Ephah;
>> all those from Sheba shall come.
> They shall bring gold and frankincense,
>> and shall proclaim the praise of the LORD.
> All the flocks of Kedar shall be gathered to you,
>> the rams of Nebaioth shall minister to you;
> they shall be acceptable on my altar,
>> and I will glorify my glorious house. (Isa 60:1–7)

The difference is that, in Matthew, the magi are not attracted by the fame of a building made by human hands – it is Herod who is in Jerusalem – but rather by the witness of a star. In Jesus's case, the heavens themselves point to his glory.

Most importantly, by thus structuring the messianic genealogy, Matthew points out that Jesus's life is not only in continuity with the divine promises to Abraham and to David, but also in complete identification with the reality representing the repetition of Genesis 3 – namely, the exile. The evangelist therefore portrays Jesus's birth exactly at the crossroads between God's faithfulness and human failure.

What is more, Matthew occasionally breaks the overall pattern of Jesus's genealogy and mentions four women among the multitude of male names: Tamar, Rahab, Ruth, and Bathsheba (Matt 1:3, 5, 6). These women are never depicted pejoratively by the evangelist, and some of them are in fact models of trust in God in the Jewish Scriptures. But each of these female figures evokes a specific episode in Israel's long narrative which reminds Matthew's readers that, while the nation's biography has never been flawless and much less "perfectly pure" in nationalistic terms, God remained utterly committed to his saving purposes. The mention of Tamar takes us back to the moment when Judah, the "great" forefather of the royal tribe of Israel, (almost) epically fails to act according to God's justice with regards to his own daughter-in-law (Gen 38:1–30); and Bathsheba, who is intentionally referred to in the Greek text as "the wife of Uriah" (Matt 1:6), was the one taken by King David at the cost of her husband's life (2 Sam 11:1–12:23). The non-Israelite Rahab, for her part, was the prostitute of Jericho who helped some Israelite spies and hence was spared from destruction (Josh 2:1–24); and Ruth was a Moabite widow who showed more loyalty to God than some of her (Israelite) contemporaries in the book of Judges (Ruth 1–4).

In short, even though Jesus is the King of Israel par excellence, he did not come to write a story "from scratch," jettisoning the previous trajectory of his people. Quite the contrary: being the ultimate descendant of David and of Abraham, he embraces the story of Israel in its entirety – its failures, its falls, and its frustration – in order finally to overcome the problem of sin, chaos, and death. It therefore makes perfect sense that the angel commands Joseph to call the soon-to-be-born Messiah "Jesus" – "for he will save his people from their sins" (Matt 1:21). The name "Jesus" comes from the Aramaic term meaning "YHWH saves." Jesus is our savior, the one who came to rescue us from underneath the rubble of our broken history, so as to reverse the reality of Genesis 3 and to break the path to new life. As Francis Watson points out, Jesus can save his people from their sins because he actually invaded the reality permeated by the sins of his own people and encountered humanity in the debris of their own transgressions.[4] To use another metaphor, Jesus picks up the baton of human vocation where all of his predecessors have dropped it, bringing it to the finish line without stumbling in autonomy.

It is unsurprising, then, that Jesus, too, was called out of Egypt (Matt 2:19–23; cf. Hos 11:1) and subsequently started his ministry not only by passing through the waters (Matt 3:13–17; cf. Exod 14:15–25), but also by

---

4. Watson, *Fourfold Gospel*, 42.

being declared God's Son (Matt 3:17; cf. Exod 4:22; Ps 2:7) before being led by the divine presence into the desert (Matt 4:1; cf. Exod 16:35). Further, having wandered for forty days and forty nights in the wilderness, Jesus thoroughly resists following his own knowledge of "good and evil." When tempted to use his authority to affirm his divine sonship, he quotes from an appropriate passage of the law: "One does not live by bread alone, but by every word that comes from the mouth of God" (Matt 4:4; cf. Deut 8:3). As the one finally carrying out God's plan to restore the cosmos, Jesus relives Israel's history to perfection, living out the human vocation according to the Creator's standards.

With all this in mind, we can now see why Jesus is so important besides his death on the cross. Jesus's sacrifice for our sins could only be accepted by God as a sufficient and definitive act because Jesus perfectly recapitulated the human vocation, as our ultimate representative. Jesus is the one who placed himself at the intersection between the human fallen-from-grace condition and God's desire to restore us, making this intersection into a safe way towards the redemption of heaven and earth. Jesus was the one who did what Adam and Eve – and all of us, including Israel – were unable to do, enabling what was necessary for God to dwell in his cosmic temple. We need Jesus because he is the head of a new humanity, our champion, and the climax of the plot of salvation. To be saved, then, is to understand that Jesus is the only savior.

But how exactly did Jesus accomplish these things? His contemporaries expected very specific deeds from the Messiah. Would Jesus live up to those aspirations? More to the point, if everyone else in the biblical story failed to live up to God's character, how did Jesus succeed? What else is important for us to understand about his identity? These are the subjects of the next few chapters. For now, we must assimilate the fundamental truth that gives meaning to the good news of Jesus Christ: he is our final representative before the Creator God – our champion, "the pioneer and perfecter of our faith" (Heb 12:2). It is Jesus we can trust; it is him we must follow.

12

God's Image Restored: The Kingdom of God Has Come

Now after John was arrested, Jesus came to Galilee, proclaiming the good news of God, and saying, "The time is fulfilled, and the kingdom of God has come near; repent, and believe in the good news." (Mark 1:14–15)

Jesus of Nazareth is the turning point in the plot of salvation. The long-awaited Messiah and ideal Davidic-Abrahamic descendant – the ultimate representative of humanity – stood in the intersection between our failure and God's faithfulness to pave the way for the redemption of heaven and earth. The great eighteenth-century hymn writer Charles Wesley expresses the thrust of the first Christmas well in his magnificent hymn "Come, Thou Long Expected Jesus":

> Come, thou long expected Jesus
> Born to set thy people free;
> From our fears and sins release us,
> Let us find our rest in thee.
> Israel's strength and consolation,
> Hope of all the earth thou art;
> Dear desire of every nation,
> Joy of every longing heart
>
> Born thy people to deliver,
> Born a child and yet a king,
> Born to reign in us forever,
> Now thy gracious kingdom bring.

By thine own eternal spirit
Rule in all our hearts alone;
By thine own sufficient merit
Raise us to thy glorious throne.

But how exactly was the Messiah to deliver his people? It is not uncommon for me to run into Christians who are used to describing the ministry of Jesus in terms of qualities such as love, forgiveness, or compassion. If we attend to the first three gospels, however, we find the unambiguous definition of the Messiah's mission under the rubric of the kingdom of God. The Gospel of Mark is a classic example, as it introduces Jesus's activities in Galilee with the programmatic summary of his preaching: "the kingdom of God has come near" (Mark 1:15).

The question that follows concerns what this crucial theme is about. While the kingdom of God is often associated with the word "heaven" and regarded as a "spiritual" place where believers go after they die, the biblical theme of the divine dominion over the world cannot be more distant from the supposedly "ethereal" heaven which dominates popular imagination. Throughout the Scriptures, the language of the kingdom of God is connected to the hope for the reestablishment of God's cosmic order through the resumption of human vocation. This reality is particularly epitomized in the Davidic kingship. As we have seen, Psalm 2 is explicit about this idea: YHWH's rule finds its visible expression in the Israelite throne, on which sits the one called "my anointed one" and "my son" by the Sovereign of the universe. The vision of Daniel 7, wherein the restoration of the chosen nation is closely tied to the vindication of their representative, is another important instance of this notion: "the people of the holy ones of the Most High" are depicted as a truly human figure (one like a human being [or "son of man," NRSV margin] unlike the beastly leaders of the pagan empires), and they are the ones who receive from "the Ancient One" an everlasting kingdom. More relevant still is the fact that this kingdom represents the kingdom of God himself:

To him was given dominion
    and glory and kingship,
that all peoples, nations, and languages
    should serve him.
His dominion is an everlasting dominion
    that shall not pass away,
and his kingship is one
    that shall never be destroyed. . . .

The kingship and dominion
> and the greatness of the kingdoms under the whole heaven
> shall be given to the people of the holy ones of the Most
> > High;
their kingdom shall be an everlasting kingdom,
> and all dominions shall serve and obey them. (Dan 7:14, 27)

In fact, by the time the prophets began to announce hope for the future when the exile was imminent, they deployed this same language, affirming that God's final rule over the world would culminate in the renewal of the harmony lost in Eden (cf. Isa 11:1–11).

The kingdom of God is all about the will of the Supreme King being done on earth as it is in heaven, in contrast to human autonomy since Adam and Eve. The Greek word *basilea*, translated as "kingdom," connotes a dimension where a king exerts his authority. By defining Jesus's mission in these terms, therefore, the evangelists are shouting to us that this Jesus – the Messiah, the perfect descendant of David and of Abraham – inaugurates this reality. Such is the reason for Jesus's teaching his followers to pray precisely in these terms: "Your kingdom come. Your will be done, on earth as it is in heaven" (Matt 6:10). God's kingdom is his will being done, "on earth as it is in heaven."

No wonder Jesus is also called Son of God and Son of Man in all four gospels. Simply put, the former places the identity of Jesus in continuity with Israel's vocation as well as with the story of David (cf. Exod 4:22; 2 Sam 7:14; Ps 2:7), whereas the latter suggests the ushering in of the everlasting kingdom in the pattern of Daniel 7. (There are other reasons for the use of such terms, but we need not unpack them here.) The prominence of the kingdom of God theme in Jesus's ministry underscores the inauguration of the time dreamed of by the prophets – the moment when YHWH would resume his reign over the cosmos. As N. T. Wright eloquently puts it: "This means, of course, that the announcement of the kingdom of god could never, in the nature of the case, be heard as a 'timeless' message, an incidental example or occurrence of some general truth. The whole point of it was that Israel's dream was coming true *right now*."[1]

---

1. N. T. Wright, *Victory of God*, 228 (emphasis original). This also explains the importance of John the Baptist, who in all four gospels is the forerunner of the Messiah and anticipates the coming of the kingdom of God in Jesus. To quote from Wright again, "Jesus regarded the work of John as the launching-pad for his own work, and it is historically probable that he saw John's arrest as the appropriate time to begin his own independent career of kingdom-proclamation" (Ibid.).

At this point, then, it is crucial to understand that the things Jesus teaches have little to do with "moral lessons" intended to make us "better" or "more religious" people. The words of Jesus are not mere "spiritual truths" that supposedly help us to live at peace with ourselves. In the same vein, Jesus's mighty deeds are far removed from the folkloric notion that he simply wanted to show off his power to the public. All that Jesus says and accomplishes concerns the arrival of the kingdom of God, the restoration of the order of the cosmos, and the resumption of YHWH's will as the central element defining the identity of his people.

In his most famous sermon, Jesus explains what the righteousness of the kingdom of God consists of, and claims, rather astonishingly: "Do not think that I have come to abolish the law or the prophets; I have come not to abolish but to fulfill" (Matt 5:17). The theme of fulfillment comes from the Greek word *plērōma*, which often carries the sense of bringing something to its culmination. One of the foremost roles of "the law and the prophets" was to express YHWH's character, in the light of which humanity had been called to live since the garden of Eden. Hence, by fulfilling "the law and the prophets," Jesus manifests once and for all the very reality which the Scriptures have pointed to: "Be perfect . . . as your heavenly Father is perfect" (Matt 5:48). At the end of this homily, in fact, Jesus gives the same life-and-death weight to his words as YHWH had given to the terms of the covenant in Deuteronomy 28:

> Not everyone who says to me, "Lord, Lord," will enter the kingdom of heaven, but only the one who does the will of my Father in heaven. On that day many will say to me, "Lord, Lord, did we not prophesy in your name, and cast out demons in your name, and do many deeds of power in your name?" Then I will declare to them, "I never knew you; go away from me, you evildoers."
>
> Everyone then who hears these words of mine and acts on them will be like a wise man who built his house on rock. The rain fell, the floods came, and the winds blew and beat on that house, but it did not fall, because it had been founded on rock. And everyone who hears these words of mine and does not act on them will be like a foolish man who built his house on sand. The rain fell, and the floods came, and the winds blew and beat against that house, and it fell – and great was its fall! (Matt 7:21–27)

Jesus's teaching is the clear – incarnate – exposition of YHWH's way of life. Listening to and obeying him is nonnegotiable for the subjects of the King of the cosmos.

Given this, it is unsurprising that Jesus performs so many healings and exorcisms. The signs accompanying his mission are not ends in themselves – by definition, signs point to greater realities (an important point that the Gospel of John underscores). Jesus's healings and exorcisms, though surely bearing a rich diversity of theological implications, are in fundamental continuity with the need for the restoration of God's image in humanity, previously outlined in the biblical story. This is what the Creator has been looking forward to since Genesis 3: the redemption of the cosmos would be achieved through the salvation of those created in the image of the King of the universe.

But sin has damaged humanity in such a way that all of us have to some degree come to resemble the gods we have worshiped. (Gollum from *The Lord of the Rings* is the perfect portrait of human nature alienated from the divine presence.) Like statues, we have ears, but don't grasp the truth; we have eyes, but don't perceive the divine grace; we have mouths, but don't proclaim the glory of God; we have limbs, but don't use them to serve our Creator; we have hearts, but don't follow wisdom (cf. Ps 115:1–11; Isa 6:9–10).

It seems by no means irrelevant, then, that the evangelists tell us of Jesus addressing very specific kinds of illnesses: blindness, deafness, muteness, lameness, and issues of ceremonial purity, such as bleeding and skin conditions. (Demons appear to fall into the last category as well, since they are referred to as "unclean spirits.") As signs pointing to broader truths, therefore, Jesus's healings and exorcisms herald the start of God's definitive work of restoration among his people. The prophet Isaiah had envisaged the day of divine visitation in precisely these terms:

> Say to those who are of a fearful heart,
>   "Be strong, do not fear!
> Here is your God.
>   He will come with vengeance,
> with terrible recompense.
>   He will come and save you."
>
> Then the eyes of the blind shall be opened,
>   and the ears of the deaf unstopped;
> then the lame shall leap like a deer,
>   and the tongue of the speechless sing for joy.
> For waters shall break forth in the wilderness,
>   and streams in the desert. (Isa 35:4–6)

The kingdom of God, then, is all about the image of God being restored among his people.[2]

The choice of the twelve apostles in the context where God's kingdom is preached in Galilee seems to corroborate this emphasis (cf. Mark 3:13–29). The twelve disciples parallel the twelve tribes of Israel, originally appointed by YHWH to be vehicles of his revelation to the nations. These Jewish apostles now stand for the eschatological chosen nation, shaped in the likeness of the Messiah. Evidently, Jesus came not only to die, but also to call a people to follow – and to look like – him.

Before we proceed any further, there is one serious hurdle that Jesus has to face. First-century Jews had particular expectations of what the Messiah should achieve. According to some Jewish texts dating from a period close to Jesus's time, the eschatological king would purify Jerusalem by organizing a powerful army to cast the pagan presence out of the land (cf. Psalms of Solomon 17). And, though Jesus attracts the admiration of many, he does not fit into some of his contemporaries' categories. For instance, not only does he come from the insignificant village of Nazareth (cf. John 1:45–46), but Jesus also insists that the kingdom of God is available to anyone who trusts the Messiah, including those regarded as unworthy by the religious elite (cf. Mark 2:13–17). More importantly, far from planning a military revolution, the Messiah of the gospels announces that the climax of his mission will take place on a cross (Mark 8:31–33). As a result, in addition to being rejected by the nation's authorities, Jesus ends up being abandoned by his own followers.

Accordingly, the kingdom of God is both accessible and shut: accessible to anyone who, recognizing his or her own bankruptcy before God, clings to Christ (cf. Matt 5:3), but shut to those who consider themselves rich from the standpoint of divine justice. And, at one point, Jesus begins to teach in parables, whose purpose is to provoke careful reflection and thus to separate genuine disciples from casual listeners. This is precisely what is implied in the programmatic parable of the sower, which speaks of Jesus's preaching of the kingdom: while the gospel is sown in all kinds of soil, only those who truly welcome the word bear fruit (Mark 4:1–20). Furthermore, Jesus begins to speak in parables only after being publicly rejected by some prominent representatives of the Jerusalem elite (Mark 3:20–30). When explaining to his disciples why he speaks in "mysteries," Jesus compares his own generation with the stubborn Israelites of Isaiah's days: those, too, having ears, did not

---

2. I am grateful to Rikk Watts for stressing this in his classes at Regent College.

understand; having eyes, did not perceive; and, having hearts, did not believe (Mark 4:10–12; cf. Isa 6:9–10).

For these reasons, the gospel bears from the outset a strong sense of urgency: "The time is fulfilled, and the kingdom of God has come near; repent, and believe in the good news" (Mark 1:15). Repentance is the necessary response to such a momentous event. The Greek term *metanoia* connotes a "mind changing," and the equivalent Hebrew verb *šûḇ* means "to turn" or "to change direction." In sum, because the reign of YHWH is already present, conversion is imperative: to see all reality through the new lens of the gospel and to give up projecting our own idolatrous desires onto the Creator. This is how the kingdom of God reaches us: Jesus fully embodies the character of God and calls us to have the Creator's image restored through following the Messiah. To be saved is "to turn" unreservedly to our end-time King, knowing that his rule is secured by his "own sufficient merit."

13

He Heals the Leper, Forgives Sins, and Silences the Storm? The Authority of the Messiah

And the Word became flesh and lived among us, and we have seen his glory, the glory as of a father's only son, full of grace and truth. (John 1:14)

In the last two chapters, we began to describe the core of Jesus's mission: he came to reverse the problem of human autonomy, establishing the kingdom of God among the nations. The Messiah took upon himself the fallen history of his people, and lived Israel's vocation to its fullness – in him, the divine will is done "on earth as it is in heaven."

But the more curious reader may wish to ask an uncomfortable question at this point. When we spoke of the exile in the tenth chapter, we noted that the reality of sin has proven insurmountable for the sons and daughters of Adam and Eve. Paul gives no room for doubting this: "sin came into the world through one man, and death came through sin, and so death spread to all because all have sinned" (Rom 5:12). If Jesus was indeed like one of us, how did he manage to fulfill "the law and the prophets"? How is it possible for anyone to overcome the reality of Genesis 3?

Many Christians sometimes forget this, but none of Jesus's contemporaries questioned his flesh-and-blood-ness. No one, anywhere in the gospels, ever wastes their time analyzing "the stuff" Jesus was made of. His fellow Nazarenes, in fact, sarcastically ask about his origins when he claims to be Israel's end-time liberator: "Is not this Joseph's son?" (Luke 4:16–22; cf. Isa 61:1–2). Only an ordinary man would sound that laughable! It is imperative to emphasize that the Messiah of the New Testament is fully human: Jesus would feel hunger and thirst, get tired, suffer from bodily and emotional pain, smile at beautiful things, and enjoy a good meal with his friends and family. Jesus would even suffer from a stench in his armpits after the long journeys his itinerant ministry demanded. Indeed, someone who ends his career crushed by the oppressive logic of the Roman Empire, nailed to a torture device reserved for the worst kind of criminal, must be human like any of us. A "spiritual" or angelic being would never have suffered like him. Jesus was fully human, full stop.

This is why the author of the Johannine Epistles scolds some heretics in Asia Minor at the end of the first century who were influenced by a form of Greek dualism and taught that Christ's sufferings, not least his death, had happened only "in appearance." (This doctrine assumed the supposed superiority of "spiritual" realities over matter, and came to be known as Docetism – a term deriving from the Greek word *dókēsis*, meaning "appearance.") John is blunt regarding this: since the apostolic message concerns "what we have heard, what we have seen with our eyes, what we have looked at and touched with our hands, concerning the word of life" (1 John 1:1), to deny that "Jesus Christ has come in the flesh" is to align oneself with "the deceiver and the antichrist" (2 John 7).

And yet, this indisputably human Jesus makes some staggering claims regarding his authority. One of the most perplexing things in the canonical gospels is Jesus's assuming of prerogatives that belong to the Creator, the God of Israel. In the Sermon on the Mount, for example, Jesus does not derive the thrust of his words from anyone but himself. Instead of speaking in the name of YHWH, prefacing his statements with the prophetic adage "thus says the LORD," the Messiah reconfigures the meaning of "the law and the prophets" according to his own authority: "You have heard that it was said to those of ancient times . . . but I say to you . . ." (Matt 5:21–48). In other places, particularly in John's gospel, Jesus not only suggests his preexistence, but also associates his identity with images that are attributed to YHWH in the Scriptures: "Very truly, I tell you, before Abraham was, I am" (John 8:58), and "I am the good shepherd" (John 10:11; cf. Ps 23:1).

So while some listeners respond with initial excitement, others take deep offense at his claims. I have to admit that, if I had been a Jew in the first century, I myself would have probably had an ambivalent attitude towards him. Who does this son of a carpenter think he is! We must agree with C. S. Lewis that the person remaining indifferent to Jesus has never considered the force of what Jesus really says:

I am trying here to prevent anyone saying the really foolish thing that people often say about Him: I'm ready to accept Jesus as a great moral teacher, but I don't accept his claim to be God. That is the one thing we must not say. A man who was merely a man and said the sort of things Jesus said would not be a great moral teacher. He would either be a lunatic – on the level with the man who says he is a poached egg – or else he would be the Devil of Hell. You must make your choice. Either this man was, and is, the Son of God, or else a madman or something worse. You can shut him up for a fool, you can spit at him and kill him as a demon or you can fall at his feet and call him Lord and God, but let us not come with any patronizing nonsense about his being a great human teacher. He has not left that open to us.[1]

Had Jesus only *said* such seemingly absurd things, we would have good reason not to take him seriously. What takes away the breath of his original audience, however, is not just what comes out of Jesus's mouth, but most forcefully what he *does*. Here are three examples, extracted from Mark, the earliest written gospel.

Mark 1:40–42 records one of the first healings Jesus performs during his ministry in Galilee:

A leper came to him begging him, and kneeling he said to him, "If you choose, you can make me clean." Moved with pity, Jesus stretched out his hand and touched him, and said to him, "I do choose. Be made clean!" Immediately the leprosy left him, and he was made clean.

In the Old Testament, we find many accounts of the sick being visited by God's mercy, and Jesus did not invent therapeutic activities such as the one presented in Mark. One recalls the healing of Naaman, who was cured of leprosy in the days of Elisha (cf. 2 Kgs 5:1–19) and thus offers a precedent for what happens in the gospels.

What seems unprecedented is the specific dynamic of the healing of the leper in Mark. According to the Leviticus code, leprosy was not necessarily a sinful condition, but a sign of the dysfunctional nature of the world after Genesis 3. This is the rationale behind the disease's falling into the category of impurity: it reflected the effect of the chaos and death that were absent in Eden. More to the point, the Messiah is never portrayed in the sources as

---

1. Lewis, *Mere Christianity*, 52.

being expected to cure leprosy with his bare hands. In Jewish tradition about that time, there was an anticipation that only YHWH could bring definitive purification among the people (cf. Leviticus Rabbah 15:9). And that event was reserved for the "last days," when everything associated with chaos and death would be reversed by the divine presence.[2] But Jesus purifies the leper at will: "I do choose. Be made clean!" Mark appears to find it unnecessary to spell out all the implications of this event, but the informed reader can hasten to ask: Who is this one, who touches the leper and cleanses him by his own authority?

In Mark 2:1–12, moreover, we see the famous story of a paralyzed man who, in addition to being cured by Jesus, also has his sins forgiven:

> When he returned to Capernaum after some days, it was reported that he was at home. So many gathered around that there was no longer room for them, not even in front of the door; and he was speaking the word to them. Then some people came, bringing to him a paralyzed man, carried by four of them. And when they could not bring him to Jesus because of the crowd, they removed the roof above him; and after having dug through it, they let down the mat on which the paralytic lay. When Jesus saw their faith, he said to the paralytic, "Son, your sins are forgiven." Now some of the scribes were sitting there, questioning in their hearts, "Why does this fellow speak in this way? It is blasphemy! Who can forgive sins but God alone?" At once Jesus perceived in his spirit that they were discussing these questions among themselves; and he said to them, "Why do you raise such questions in your hearts? Which is easier, to say to the paralytic, 'Your sins are forgiven,' or to say, 'Stand up and take your mat and walk'? But so that you may know that the Son of Man has authority on earth to forgive sins" – he said to the paralytic – "I say to you, stand up, take your mat and go to your home." And he stood up, and immediately took the mat and went out before all of them; so that they were all amazed and glorified God, saying, "We have never seen anything like this!"

The dialogue between Jesus and his interlocutors is intriguing. Impressed by the faith of the people who have just brought their lame friend down through the roof so that Jesus could see him, the Messiah approaches the paralytic and says that his sins are forgiven. The scribes, however, object with a thoroughly

---

2. See the second chapter in Thiessen, *Jesus and the Forces of Death*, titled "Jesus in a World of Ritual Impurity" (Kindle loc. 663–1069).

orthodox (and commonsensical) statement: "Who can forgive sins but God alone?" Indeed, to a common first-century Jew, forgiveness of sins was one of the many prerogatives which pertained to YHWH alone, so much so that Jesus refuses to rebuke the scribes for their answer – obviously, no one can forgive sins except the Creator, the God of Israel. And yet, Jesus proceeds to pose a riddle to his listeners: "Which is easier, to say to the paralytic, 'Your sins are forgiven,' or to say, 'Stand up and take your mat and walk'?"

The point is that neither of these – whether forgiving sins or healing the paralytic – is "easy" for us mortal human beings. But by his own authority Jesus commands the paralytic to walk, with the result that the healing attests the truth of what Jesus has previously claimed: the Son of Man really does have "authority on earth to forgive sins." And, again, the end-time liberator of the nation was not expected to do any of this. What does this suggest about Jesus?

Furthermore, in Mark 4:35–41, there is another well-known passage where Jesus once again accomplishes something unexpected. In this case, it is the very forces of creation that are tamed before the disciples' eyes:

> On that day, when evening had come, he said to them, "Let us go across to the other side." And leaving the crowd behind, they took him with them in the boat, just as he was. Other boats were with him. A great windstorm arose, and the waves beat into the boat, so that the boat was already being swamped. But he was in the stern, asleep on the cushion; and they woke him up and said to him, "Teacher, do you not care that we are perishing?" He woke up and rebuked the wind, and said to the sea, "Peace! Be still!" Then the wind ceased, and there was a dead calm. He said to them, "Why are you afraid? Have you still no faith?" And they were filled with great awe and said to one another, "Who then is this, that even the wind and the sea obey him?"

As with the previous examples, signs of this nature are not novel in the Jewish tradition. We have already seen many instances in which YHWH exerts his sovereign rule over the brutal (to humans) forces of creation. The exodus is the most emblematic event of this kind. What is startling about Mark 4:35–41 is, again, the person performing the sign. The disciples think they are about to die, because the sea and the storm evoke the forces of chaos that are beyond human control. The fact that, elsewhere, YHWH addresses Job out of the storm, for example, connotes God's sovereignty over nature, which humanity cannot tame (cf. Job 38:1). When the disciples hurry to wake Jesus up, therefore, they most likely expect him to ask God for deliverance. (The resemblance with the

Jonah story, wherein the captain of the sinking boat wakes the prophet up and pleads with him to pray, is amusing indeed!)

Once Jesus is up from his nap, however, he never kneels down, nor does he make a petition to God in heaven. He directly addresses both the sea and the storm, by uttering two imperatives: "Peace! Be still!" – or, literally, "Silence! Be quiet!" The most frightening thing is that both the sea and the storm obey Jesus's commands. The disciples are Jews, familiar with their sacred texts. They know who in the plot of salvation is the only one able to do what this son of a carpenter just did: YHWH, whose Spirit hovered over the waters before the creation of the cosmos, who parted the sea so that the Israelites could come out of Egypt to God's new creation, through the exodus. As my former teacher Rikk Watts used to insist in his classes, this explains why the disciples end up being more afraid of Jesus than of the storm which had threatened their lives just a few moments ago: "Who then is this, that even the wind and the sea obey him?"

As we pay close attention to the gospels' portrayal of Jesus's mighty deeds, then, we realize that this human being called Jesus of Nazareth – who suckled at his mother's breasts for the earliest months of his life, needed someone to change his diaper (or the equivalent of that in antiquity), cried many times from hunger and sleep and gas, stumbled on his first walking attempts, learned to speak Aramaic, Hebrew, and some Greek, assimilated the typical accent of his village, studied the Scriptures, submitted to the authority of his parents, dealt with some bully classmates at school (or the equivalent of that in antiquity), cut himself when learning to shave, cried while chopping onions, breathed the dusty air of first-century Palestine, practiced his prayers before meals, saw Joseph and Mary work hard to pay their taxes, had countless moments of boredom and frustration, washed his feet before bed, was saddened by the injustices of the world, and finished his mission being executed on a rugged cross by the Romans – must be perceived in close identification with the God of the biblical plot of salvation. Jesus was, inexplicably, the manifestation of YHWH's presence among his people. In Jesus, the God who created the heavens and earth, called Abraham, ransomed Israel, gave the law, made a covenant with David, and announced through the prophets the restoration of the cosmos, revealed himself in flesh and blood.

What Matthew says about the birth of Joseph's adopted son, in the light of a prophecy from Isaiah, is best taken literally: "'Look, the virgin shall conceive and bear a son, and they shall name him Emmanuel,' which means, 'God is with us'" (Matt 1:23; cf. Isa 7:14; 8:8–10). Jesus is "God with us" in the most concrete sense of the term. This person who came to fulfill the role of the people's ideal king – the perfect human being, the long-awaited descendant of David, of Abraham, and of Eve – is none other than the Creator himself who, since Genesis 3, has revealed his character to humanity and worked to make the cosmos his ultimate dwelling place. Jesus is the very Creator who came to us as the new Adam. In Jesus, the great Author of the plot of salvation enters the drama which he himself has written.

Accordingly, John the evangelist explicitly speaks of Jesus as God incarnate: "And the Word became flesh and lived among us, and we have seen his glory, the glory as of a father's only son, full of grace and truth" (John 1:14). The Greek verb translated as "lived" is *skēnoō*, "to reside in a tent," which the Septuagint consistently uses to refer to the tabernacle, where the glory of YHWH dwelled among his people. Hence, because the Word "tabernacled" among the disciples, they saw his "glory." What is more, such "glory" was the visible expression of the character of YHWH revealed at Sinai in Exodus 34:6: "full of grace and truth."[3] The key difference, of course, is that Moses received only a "spoken portrait" of God, whereas in Jesus of Nazareth we behold the very face of YHWH.

Jesus not only fully relives the story of his people, but also (and at the same time) reveals God's glory to humanity. Because of him, no one has ever again to remain in the dark as to who God is: "in him was life, and the life was the light of all people" (John 1:4). Jesus the Messiah is all we need to contemplate the face of the Creator God. A great mystery is thus unveiled to us. In the event of the incarnation, we see the end to which the Creator designed us: that we should be like him. When God's grace makes us human as Jesus, it transforms us into God's own likeness.

Before moving on to the next chapter, we must note one curious aspect in the gospels. As much as Jesus says and does all these amazing things, not even his closest disciples fully grasp – or perhaps accept – the implications of Jesus's distinguished authority. During Jesus's ministry, no one goes around proclaiming that he is the God of Israel made human. And the reason is fairly simple: it has never crossed the disciples' minds – or anyone's, really – that YHWH would manifest himself in flesh and blood, in the person of his Messiah.

Consequently, as sensational as it may have been to witness all the signs performed by Jesus, Peter and his friends did not have the categories adequate to interpret the consequences of such a revelation. The evangelists tell us about Jesus in retrospect, but at the moment those things were happening the only way the disciples could react was by asking, "Who on earth is this?" And the aggravating factor was that Jesus's crucifixion seemed to contradict

---

3. See further discussion in Bauckham, 43–53.

whatever positive conclusions the disciples had drawn regarding his identity. It was already impossible to accept the notion of a crucified Messiah, as the episode in Caesarea Philippi indicates (cf. Mark 8:31–33). How much more ludicrous would have sounded the idea of a Roman cross as the place where YHWH demonstrated his ultimate act of self-giving love? Only on the third day following Jesus's death, after his resurrection, would his followers finally understand.

14

The Defeat of Death: The Messiah's Final Enemy

Then Jesus, again greatly disturbed, came to the tomb. It was a cave, and a stone was lying against it. Jesus said, "Take away the stone." Martha, the sister of the dead man, said to him, "Lord, already there is a stench because he has been dead four days." Jesus said to her, "Did I not tell you that if you believed, you would see the glory of God?" So they took away the stone. And Jesus looked upward and said, "Father, I thank you for having heard me. I knew that you always hear me, but I have said this for the sake of the crowd standing here, so that they may believe that you sent me." When he had said this, he cried with a loud voice, "Lazarus, come out!" The dead man came out, his hands and feet bound with strips of cloth, and his face wrapped in a cloth. Jesus said to them, "Unbind him, and let him go." (John 11:38–44)

A couple of chapters back, we saw that first-century Jews had specific expectations about what the Messiah should accomplish. One of the most important of these was the definitive defeat of Israel's enemies, in the pattern of what King David had achieved in the monarchic period. That is to say, the final reversal of the reality of exile would take place in the emancipation of the chosen people from the hands of the Romans, with the restoration of the Davidic throne and the temple worship at the center of their identity. From that point on, all the nations of the earth would see YHWH's righteousness, for better or for worse.

It is not difficult to understand why biblical characters such as David would so deeply inspire the popular imagination in the first century. He had defeated Goliath, expelled the pagan oppressors from the land, and unified the nation under the covenant. So, naturally, Jesus's contemporaries would often picture the eschatological ruler as a military commander, under whose auspices the Romans would be cast out of Palestine and an era of perennial stability would be ushered in. (The Maccabees a century or so before seem to have taken upon themselves a similar task, but their non-Davidic pedigree eventually occasioned considerable disapproval from stricter circles.) Indeed, by the turn of the Christian era, Palestinian Jews had already witnessed the emergence of messianic movements trying to attain national independence by violent means. The simple fact that Jesus's disciples recognize him as the Messiah (cf. Matt 16:13–20) must lead us to ask precisely how he interprets his mission in relation to such hopes.

But, again, the gospels offer a significant qualification to what Jesus does as Israel's end-time King. The most basic truth to be highlighted is that the gospels do not portray Jesus as a guerrilla warrior. His teachings are diametrically opposed to violence, to the point that his disciples are told to pray for their persecutors (Matt 5:7, 9–12, 38–48). The Messiah also radically contradicts the strife for hegemony. When offered the possibility of establishing the kingdom of God by force, in fact, Jesus compares such an idea to idolatry: "Away with you, Satan! for it is written, 'Worship the Lord your God, and serve only him'" (Matt 4:10).

That said, it is equally wrong to conclude that Jesus came to bring about a "spiritual" kingdom. In most occurrences in the New Testament, the Greek term *pneumatikos*, translated as "spiritual," suggests the influence of the Holy Spirit, not a dimension (supposedly) superior to the visible, concrete world. "Spiritual," in other words, is someone or something which is under the holy effect of the Spirit of God. Most importantly, the evangelists never define the kingdom of God in abstract terms. Jesus teaches his followers to pray: "Your kingdom come. Your will be done, on earth as it is in heaven" (Matt 6:10). What is more, a key aspect of the kingdom's ethic is the generosity of the rich to the poor, and Jesus himself spends a lot of his time restoring the most basic earthly conditions of the needy: as we have seen, his healing of the sick points to God's purpose of making his people whole again. Accordingly, on Jesus's lips, the term "kingdom" makes sense only when understood concretely, as the space where the King's will is carried out. Jesus's refusal of a militaristic agenda has nothing to do with an alleged interest in a "spiritual" (meaning "ethereal") dimension.

How, then, does Jesus interpret his mission in relation to his contemporaries' hopes for deliverance? We must recall that one of the most essential activities within Jesus's ministry is his casting out of demons. Among many other things, the exorcisms provide proof that God's kingdom has indeed arrived: "But if it is by the Spirit of God that I cast out demons, then the kingdom of God has come to you" (Matt 12:28). The anticipation of the Messiah's dealing with unclean spirits, to be sure, does not figure prominently in the sources.[1] What the crowds more commonly looked forward to was the end-time ruler's organizing of an anti-Rome army so as to defeat Israel's oppressors. The Romans, after all, were seen as the "demon-possessed" desecrators of the land.

But, seen in connection with Jesus's healing ministry, the exorcisms attest the reality that the kingdom of God concerns the very restoration of his people. While many of Jesus's contemporaries thought the problem of chaos to be materialized in the pagan presence in the land, the exorcisms show the same chaos as present among the descendants of Abraham. It is suggestive that Jesus casts out unclean spirits at synagogues. While his fellow Jews expected the Messiah to cleanse the land of the Romans, Jesus solves the problem by emancipating his people from the demons. N. T. Wright helps us once again:

> In particular, the exorcisms carry with them the haunting word: "If I by the finger of god cast out demons, then the kingdom of god has come upon you." This evokes the same implicit narrative: Israel's god will one day become king; the establishment of his kingdom will involve the defeat of the enemy that has held Israel captive; there are clear signs that this is now happening; therefore the kingdom is indeed breaking in. YHWH really is becoming king; Israel really is being liberated.[2]

The exorcisms, therefore, amount to the purifying effects of the kingdom presence among the people of God.

With this in mind, we can now turn to the resurrection of Lazarus. The Gospel of John has several peculiarities vis-à-vis the three other accounts of Jesus, but the most relevant for our discussion here is that, in stark contrast to Matthew, Mark, and Luke, the fourth gospel is completely lacking in any accounts of exorcisms. This is highly significant. If the other evangelists tell us that Jesus spent so much of his time confronting the forces of chaos through the casting out of demons, why does John leave this information aside?

---

1. One Jewish tradition suggests that the Son of David would be an exorcist, but this expectation would have been very slim in Jesus's day.

2. N. T. Wright, *Victory of God*, 228.

John synthesizes the theological point of the exorcisms in a single event. The fourth gospel presents the core purpose of Jesus's mission in a selection of seven signs that the Son of God performs:

> Now Jesus did many other signs in the presence of his disciples, which are not written in this book. But these are written so that you may come to believe that Jesus is the Messiah, the Son of God, and that through believing you may have life in his name. (John 20:30–31)

Within this concern, the last sign Jesus performs before entering Jerusalem for the last time is precisely the resurrection of Lazarus. The episode marks the transition between the section known as "the book of signs" (John 1–11), wherein the identity of the Messiah is disclosed, and "the book of glory" (John 12–21), which narrates the unveiling of Jesus's glory in his passion. What happens to the brother of Martha and Mary is thus the climax of all the signs Jesus performs before he enters the way to the cross. The episode with Lazarus, in other words, indicates what Jesus actually came to accomplish.

We could devote a lot of space to the exegetical details of this passage, but suffice it to highlight two points here. First, we notice a very suggestive portrait of Jesus's authority and character. His attitude towards the imminent death of his friend never fails to impress me:

> But when Jesus heard it [the news of Lazarus's illness], he said, "This illness does not lead to death; rather it is for God's glory, so that the Son of God may be glorified through it." Accordingly, though Jesus loved Martha and her sister and Lazarus, after having heard that Lazarus was ill, he stayed two days longer in the place where he was.
>
> Then after this he said to the disciples, "Let us go to Judea again." The disciples said to him, "Rabbi, the Jews were just now trying to stone you, and are you going there again?" Jesus answered, "Are there not twelve hours of daylight? Those who walk during the day do not stumble, because they see the light of this world. But those who walk at night stumble, because the light is not in them." After saying this, he told them, "Our friend Lazarus has fallen asleep, but I am going there to awaken him." The disciples said to him, "Lord, if he has fallen asleep, he will be all right." Jesus, however, had been speaking about his death, but they thought that he was referring merely to sleep. Then Jesus told

them plainly, "Lazarus is dead. For your sake I am glad I was not there, so that you may believe. But let us go to him." (John 11:4–15)

No one initially understands the reasons for Jesus's delay. In an admirable display of faith, Martha laments with disappointment: "Lord, if you had been here, my brother would not have died" (11:32). Some of those standing there agree: "Could not he who opened the eyes of the blind man have kept this man from dying?" (11:37). Had the Messiah reached Bethany just a little earlier, Lazarus could have been healed. But death – this inexorable, tyrannical force overpowering humanity ever since the sin of Adam and Eve – apparently not even Jesus (in the minds of the spectators) could solve. The tomb of Lazarus has been sealed; it is too late for Jesus to do anything.

Jesus, however, is in complete control of the situation. His delay is deliberate, so that he intentionally arrives in Bethany *after* Lazarus has passed away. And the point is precisely to make sure that nobody can cure his friend. A different plan has been premeditated.

But, in spite of this, Jesus feels the pain of those he loves:

> Now Jesus had not yet come to the village, but was still at the place where Martha had met him. The Jews who were with her in the house, consoling her, saw Mary get up quickly and go out. They followed her because they thought that she was going to the tomb to weep there. When Mary came where Jesus was and saw him, she knelt at his feet and said to him, "Lord, if you had been here, my brother would not have died." When Jesus saw her weeping, and the Jews who came with her also weeping, he was greatly disturbed in spirit and deeply moved. He said, "Where have you laid him?" They said to him, "Lord, come and see." Jesus began to weep. (John 11:30–35)

Few passages in the Bible portray Jesus's solidarity with human suffering as poignantly as the story above. The one who has not even for a millisecond lost control of history also partakes in the drama of his friends. The honor of being mentioned alongside the shortest verse in the Scriptures – "Jesus began to weep" – belongs to those mourning in front of a tomb. It is thus in the scene where the Son of God performs the greatest sign in the Gospel of John that we perceive both his power and his compassion.

The second point to be mentioned is the moment Jesus chooses to do such a climactic sign prior to his crucifixion: it is not a celebration, but rather a funeral. The Creator of heaven and earth, who made himself the ideal descendant of Abraham and of David, chooses a grave to illustrate the significance of his mission. The very first sign in the fourth gospel is actually a celebration: the wedding in Cana (2:1–12). On that occasion, Jesus turned 120 liters of water used for ceremonial purification into the most elegant wine the sommelier of the feast had ever tasted, thus indicating that the messianic kingdom represents fullness of life. Nevertheless, in order for the reality demonstrated in Cana to be fully actualized, the final enemy of the people of God – and of humanity, for that matter – must be defeated: the exile from the presence of God, the persistence of the cemetery, death itself.

The thrust of the resurrection of Lazarus is hence to show the ultimate goal of Jesus's mission: the defeat of our greatest adversary, the reversal of the consequence of autonomy from the Creator. Jesus could have hastened to Bethany so as to prevent the passing of his friend. That would have brought joy to all the family, leading them to give thanks to God. Nevertheless, by raising Lazarus from the dead, Jesus would show why he had really come to the world. In Matthew, Mark, and Luke, Jesus demonstrates the presence of the kingdom of God by casting out demons. John channels this truth by claiming that Jesus came ultimately to cast out death itself. There are no exorcisms in John because, for the "beloved disciple," only one exorcism really matters to encapsulate the meaning of Jesus's ministry: the conquest of the graveyard. This is why Jesus explains what he is about to do not as an isolated event, but rather as a portent of the "most real reality" of Genesis 3 turned upside down: "I am the resurrection and the life. Those who believe in me, even though they die, will live, and everyone who lives and believes in me will never die. Do you believe this?" (John 11:25–26).

The resurrection of Lazarus points to an infinitely greater truth. Lazarus died again. But now the end-time King himself would confront head-on the enemy which no descendant of Adam and Eve could have fought. It is no coincidence, then, that Lazarus's coming out of his tomb dovetails directly with the condemnation of Jesus by the nation's authorities: "Many of the Jews therefore, who had come with Mary and had seen what Jesus did, believed in him. But some of them went to the Pharisees and told them what he had done. . . . So from that day on they planned to put him to death" (John 11:45–46, 53). Indeed, as soon as Jesus enters Jerusalem, he tells his disciples that his impending crucifixion is the moment when his glory will be revealed: "Now is the judgment of this world; now the ruler of this world will be driven out. And I, when I am lifted up from the earth, will draw all people to myself" (12:31–32; cf. 3:14–15). That is, the same Jesus who has just raised Lazarus from the dead will crush death by laying down his own life on the cross. Through his own death, Jesus is about to defeat death once and for all. David had fought against Goliath, but only Jesus can conquer the graveyard.

This is also contemplated in Jesus's interpretation of his sufferings in the light of the Passover. John finds it unnecessary to rehearse what the other evangelists have already stated concerning this (cf. Mark 14:12–26): the passion of the Christ is YHWH's saving intervention in the new exodus, the fulfillment of the preservation of Abraham's offspring from the "angel of death" and the tyranny of chaos. Remember: in Exodus 12:1–14, the blood of the sacrificed lamb was the only element determining who would not be visited by divine judgment. Jesus chooses precisely this point as the framework for understanding the cross. Simply put, the sacrifice of the Messiah will bring about the eschatological departure from bondage, the final liberation of humanity from the clutches of death. John the Baptist's announcement of Jesus as "the Lamb of God who takes away the sin of the world" (John 1:29) has already pointed forward to this reality.[3]

With this mind, it is easier to understand why the other gospels make it so clear that "the Son of Man must undergo great suffering, and be rejected by the elders, the chief priests, and the scribes, and be killed, and after three days rise again" (Mark 8:31). Yes, the Messiah "must" die, by divine necessity, because that is the only possible way for salvation to happen. The unexpected plot twist, of course, is that the leaders of the people are to participate in this, as those who actually deliver Jesus into the hands of the Romans. To quote from the prologue of John: "He came to what was his own, and his own people did not accept him" (John 1:11). As an act of irony, moreover, the religious authorities who mock the Messiah at the foot of the cross unwittingly announce

---

3. A note of clarification about the relationship between Jesus's death and the Jewish Passover is in order. Originally, the sacrifice of the Passover lamb had no atoning connotations. For such a purpose, Israel was commanded to celebrate the Day of Atonement (cf. Lev 23:26–32). In fact, in the New Testament, it is Paul who more explicitly interprets Jesus's death through the lenses of the Day of Atonement (cf. Rom 3:25–26). In any case, it was probably around the time of the exile, when the future restoration of the chosen people was portrayed by the prophets as a "new exodus" (cf. Isa 40–55), that the Passover came to be associated with the idea of forgiveness of sins. The rationale behind this interpretation seems obvious: the breaking of the covenant had led the people into exile, so the new exodus would also represent forgiveness of sins. As mentioned above, in the fourth gospel, John the Baptist seems to assume this thought. It is nonetheless curious that, according to the Synoptic Gospels, Jesus's last supper takes place during the Passover, but he never identifies himself with the sacrificial lamb – it is the bread that symbolizes Jesus's body, and it is the wine that represents his blood (cf. Mark 14:22–25). This indicates that the gospels are not so much concerned with reducing the meaning of Jesus's death to what this or that specific element of the Jewish Passover may stand for. Rather, through his death, Jesus would fulfill the realities to which the first exodus – and, for Paul, the Day of Atonement – pointed as a whole.

the truth about Jesus's death: "He saved others; he cannot save himself" (Mark 15:31). Sin was very costly to God: it took the Messiah to die so that we could be saved and brought back to life.

Up until the previous chapter, we have seen that the Creator of the universe assumed the role of our representative and lived the human vocation perfectly, bringing Israel's story to its climax. In the resurrection of Lazarus, we see that God did all this in order to defeat death for us, so that the sentence we brought upon ourselves would be paid, once and for all, by the Author of life. What follows is that, at the cross, the Creator of the cosmos also unveiled the most sublime feature of his glory. Paul is adamant: "For while we were still weak, at the right time Christ died for the ungodly. . . . God proves his love for us in that while we still were sinners Christ died for us" (Rom 5:6, 8). In a similar vein, John states elsewhere: "In this is love, not that we loved God but that he loved us and sent his Son to be the atoning sacrifice for our sins" (1 John 4:10). And, at Calvary, God the Creator revealed the core of his character: he is self-giving love (cf. 1 John 4:8).

As previously pointed out, however, Jesus's contemporaries expected the Messiah to destroy their enemies, not to be hung on a Roman cross. Gordon Fee used to say in his classes that a "crucified Messiah" would have sounded like "burnt ice" – a laughable contradiction in terms! (Isaiah's enigmatic songs about a "suffering servant" in chapters 42–53 were never interpreted in Jesus's time with reference to the Messiah, but rather as speaking of Israel. The New Testament provides the earliest instances of messianic readings of these Isaiah songs.) Peter's consternation about the crucifixion is no doubt indicative (Mark 8:31–33), and his eventual denial of Jesus seems to have little to do with the disciple's supposed cowardice (Mark 14:66–72). John tells us that Peter cuts off the ear of an armed guard in Gethsemane (John 18:10), which shows that the former fisherman was anything but a coward (also Matt 26:31–35; Mark 14:27–31; Luke 22:31–34). Instead, Peter's refusal to defend Jesus till the end, as he had promised during the last supper, smacks of sincerity: a King who voluntarily gives himself up to die for his enemies is one Peter prefers not to hear about. The disciples abandon the Messiah because they ultimately find him perplexing.

Accordingly, the cross of Christ not only crushes our own death and discloses God's glory, but also directly confronts our distorted views of who the Creator really is. The cross denounces as idolatry our tendency to shape God into the likeness of our lust for power. The cross condemns our golden calves, the fallen expectations which our hearts project onto the Creator. And the cross reminds us that the One we were made to worship is different from the lies we invent: he is YHWH, a merciful and compassionate God, full of grace and truth, who made himself human, fulfilled our vocation, died our death, and thus modeled the kind of people he always wanted us to be. How can we respond to the death of Jesus Christ, if not by bending our knees in adoration? It is at the foot of the cross that we see what we were created for. This is salvation.

15

The Decisive Morning: The Resurrection of Jesus

But on the first day of the week, at early dawn, they came to the tomb, taking the spices that they had prepared. They found the stone rolled away from the tomb, but when they went in, they did not find the body. While they were perplexed about this, suddenly two men in dazzling clothes stood beside them. The women were terrified and bowed their faces to the ground, but the men said to them, "Why do you look for the living among the dead? He is not here, but has risen. Remember how he told you, while he was still in Galilee, that the Son of Man must be handed over to sinners, and be crucified, and on the third day rise again." Then they remembered his words, and returning from the tomb, they told all this to the eleven and to all the rest. Now it was Mary Magdalene, Joanna, Mary the mother of James, and the other women with them who told this to the apostles. But these words seemed to them an idle tale, and they did not believe them. But Peter got up and ran to the tomb; stooping and looking in, he saw the linen cloths by themselves; then he went home, amazed at what had happened. (Luke 24:1–12)

About fifteen years ago, while listening to a lecture by Gordon Fee, I heard what I still consider the best illustration for the sense of mission that Jesus's disciples acquired a few days following his crucifixion. On 6 June 1944, the world witnessed one of the most momentous events of the twentieth century. Two and a half years after the attack on Pearl Harbor, the Allied forces invaded the French region of Normandy, on what came to be known as "D-Day." The

Allies took control of one of the most strategic strongholds of the Nazis, thus preluding the regaining of freedom in Europe by planting their flags on French soil. Indeed, D-Day was so monumental that it would not even take twelve months for it to culminate in "VE Day" – namely, 8 May 1945, when Hitler's troops finally surrendered. After D-Day, there could be no doubt that the war would soon be over.

According to the book of Acts, the followers of Jesus were so deeply taken by a sense of victory that nothing could shake their confidence in the message they preached – not even the many difficulties they had to face for belonging to the Messiah, including the real prospect of execution. Such boldness, moreover, was animated by the fact that the more opposition the Jesus movement suffered, the more their community grew.

From a historical point of view, however, the picture of a triumphant people, who firmly hold their ground before Caesar's lethal machine, contrasts sharply with what we see in the concluding chapters of the canonical gospels. Matthew, Mark, Luke, and John unanimously tell us that Jesus ends his "career" completely abandoned by his would-be "henchmen." Peter, for example, is struck by a terrible existential crisis when Jesus gives himself into the hands of his enemies! Furthermore, while the disciples did not abandon Jesus only out of fear, they do actually get terrified after the crucifixion: the once-brave followers of the end-time King hide themselves, ashamed of having followed a man who ended up sentenced as a failed anti-Rome insurgent (cf. John 20:19). If the crucifixion of Jesus was the last word, the book of Acts would make no sense at all: the apostolic ministry could never have followed from Calvary alone.

So the most plausible – and intellectually honest – way of interpreting the order of events between the death of Jesus and the apostles' subsequent proclamation is to accept that something extraordinary happened halfway. Something special took place for those runaway and disillusioned disciples to become missionaries and martyrs.

And the gospels address this puzzle in the most straightforward way: according to what Jesus himself had repeatedly announced before his death, he rose from the grave on the third day after his crucifixion. As Luke tells us, on the first Sunday after Jesus's execution, some women went to the tomb in order to complete the burial procedures, but the stone was no longer sealing the entrance, and his body was absent. Two angels then appeared to them, giving a bewildering report: "Why do you look for the living among the dead? He is not here, but has risen." In brief, the one who had emptied the tomb of Lazarus was no longer among the dead. The Messiah left his own grave uninhabited.

Curiously, the gospels are very succinct in telling us about the resurrection. No space is wasted in giving us a "laboratory" explanation of the empty tomb. Scholars have struggled to make sense of such economy, but it may simply suggest that the evangelists were themselves thunderstruck by the unexpected events of that Sunday morning. That is to say, in the biblical authors' estimation, it is utterly beside the point to try to make the resurrection scientifically acceptable. Like the incarnation, which no one dares to describe mathematically, Jesus's resurrection was something unprecedented, unlike any other previously known phenomena. While the Messiah did raise some people from the dead, his own resurrection was categorically different than, say, Lazarus's. Jesus was raised from the dead once and for all, uniquely and definitively; Lazarus died again, but Jesus did not – and never will.

Actually, the most important question following Jesus's resurrection has not to do with the "how?" but rather with the "now what?" The Messiah is risen, full stop – so what are the implications? Indeed, the consequences of the empty tomb are so huge and manifold that the rest of the New Testament is essentially devoted to describing their contours. The most crucial ones will be discussed in the next chapters of this book, but here we must attend to the most fundamental point, which helps us grasp how the cross could have resulted in the emergence of the church.

Simply put, the resurrection is the historical proof that everything revealed and achieved by Christ was complete and true. We often forget this, but Jesus died as a criminal. There was absolutely nothing good in the crucifixion – it was destined mainly for runaway slaves and political insurgents. As spectacular as Jesus's words and deeds may have been, therefore, none of them would have had ultimate significance had he remained dead. If that descendant of David and of Abraham had not risen on the third day, the gospels would not even exist, there would be neither Christmas nor Christianity, and probably no one would have remembered Jesus in subsequent generations. In spite of all the indisputably impressive stories surrounding his life, Jesus would have been counted as yet another bandit among the many others crushed by the Roman Empire, whose names remain unheard of.

More to the point, if the cross was the end of the road, no one could ever claim that Jesus's death was effective in solving the problem of sin and death. The exile would still define the human condition, the cosmos would remain hostage to chaos, and heaven and earth would still be broken. To think of it, it is much more coherent to be an atheist than to consider it possible to be a Christian without accepting Jesus's resurrection. The empty tomb is not a metaphorical detail in the gospel accounts: without it, Jesus would have been a lunatic impostor, and it would be foolish to be a Christian. For the same reason, a zealous Pharisee named Saul would persecute the church for proclaiming that a crucified man was Israel's end-time King. But once Saul is found by the risen Christ, everything changes radically, so much so that, in 1 Corinthians 15:17, he attributes a cause-and-effect relationship between the truth of the gospel and the empty tomb: "If Christ has not been raised, your faith is futile and you are still in your sins."

And here is another detail: when first-century Jews heard about the resurrection, they usually interpreted the idea in connection with prophetic texts such as Ezekiel 37 and Daniel 12, with reference both to the final restoration of the people and to the defeat of the wicked "on the last day." Martha, at least, seems to have held the same belief: "I know that he will rise again in the resurrection on the last day" (John 11:24). This was likely the other motive for Saul's rage against the Christians: How dare they proclaim the resurrection if Saul – who, according to his own description of himself in Philippians 3:2–6, was the most righteous Jew of his time – did not experience God's vindication? The Romans, after all, remained well lodged in Palestine. It is instructive that, while Jesus's listeners are familiar with the concept, they are not sure what to do with the Messiah's reference to his own individual resurrection: after the transfiguration scene, some disciples questioned "what this rising from the dead [namely, the rising of the Son of Man] could mean" (Mark 9:10).

The problem, however, is that the biblical story has made it transparent that no one can blaze this path, given that no one is righteous before God (cf. Rom 3:9–20). Nobody can conquer death.

Nobody, that is, except Jesus, who against all odds was raised from the dead on the third day after his crucifixion. The empty tomb thus revealed that Jesus Christ was indeed the one and only, ever since the creation of the cosmos, over whom death could not reign. As a result, the resurrection demonstrated that Jesus had really been the ideal human being, the faithful Israelite, and it proved, in time and space, that Jesus's words and deeds were real and true: in him, God's promises to Abraham and to David were at last fulfilled, Israel's story was brought to its culmination, the new creation and the new exodus had really begun, the path of autonomy was overcome, the kingdom of God was inaugurated, the restoration of God's image in humanity was initiated, chaos was tamed, the demons were put in their proper place, and human vocation was perfectly fulfilled.

Further, if that glorious Sunday morning proved the validity of Jesus's cruciform mission, it also proved the veracity of his identity. Since the resurrection evinces Jesus's success in the perspective of God the Father, the empty tomb likewise confirms that Jesus is more than a human Messiah. This explains why Thomas, in the famous story in John 20:24–29, reacts the way he does when he sees the risen Christ:

> But Thomas (who was called the Twin), one of the twelve, was not with them when Jesus came. So the other disciples told him, "We have seen the Lord." But he said to them, "Unless I see the mark of the nails in his hands, and put my finger in the mark of the nails and my hand in his side, I will not believe."
>
> A week later his disciples were again in the house, and Thomas was with them. Although the doors were shut, Jesus came and stood among them and said, "Peace be with you." Then he said to Thomas, "Put your finger here and see my hands. Reach out your hand and put it in my side. Do not doubt but believe." Thomas answered him, "My Lord and my God!" Jesus said to him, "Have you believed because you have seen me? Blessed are those who have not seen and yet have come to believe."

With good reason, Thomas is commonly labeled an unbeliever. But we should not be too hard on him. If his colleagues are telling the truth – "We have seen the Lord" – this fact must change absolutely everything. So Thomas is theologically consistent, not merely a skeptic. Was Jesus raised from the dead? Well, then all this time the disciples have been walking with God incarnate! But this is too much to take in without some corroborating facts: "Unless I see the mark of the nails in his hands, and put my finger in the mark of the nails and my hand in his side, I will not believe." Accordingly, Jesus approaches Thomas, and sure enough the resurrection confirms the incarnation: "My Lord and my God!" At that very moment, Thomas was sure. On the cross, the eternal God had indeed defeated death, the greatest enemy of his people.

What we see in the book of Acts, then, is the assurance that, since death has been conquered by Jesus, he has assumed the highest position in the universe, as the Lord over all things. Peter spells out precisely this reality at Pentecost: "Therefore let the entire house of Israel know with certainty that God has made him both Lord and Messiah, this Jesus whom you crucified" (Acts 2:36). And so also Paul in Philippians 2:5–11:

> Let the same mind be in you that was in Christ Jesus,
>
> > who, though he was in the form of God,
> > did not regard equality with God
> > as something to be exploited,

but emptied himself,
>taking the form of a slave,
>being born in human likeness.
And being found in human form,
>he humbled himself
>and became obedient to the point of death –
>even death on a cross.

Therefore God also highly exalted him
>and gave him the name
>that is above every name,
so that at the name of Jesus
>every knee should bend,
>in heaven and on earth and under the earth,
and every tongue should confess
>that Jesus Christ is Lord,
>to the glory of God the Father.

In the light of the great plot of salvation, therefore, we see that the basic meaning of the Christian Easter is cosmic: in Jesus's empty tomb, the divine plan for the universe since creation finds its resolution. Sin has created the cemetery, but Christ has remedied this problem. The gospel is the event in which God invaded time and space in the person of the Messiah, conquered death for us, and took absolute lordship over all things in the universe. Genesis 3 has been solved, the exile has finally been overcome. According to G. K. Beale, as first-century Jews hoped for the resurrection at the end of history, Jesus's rising from the dead indicated the beginning of "the end of times."[1] Or, as N. T. Wright notes: "When Jesus rose from the dead on Easter morning, he rose as the beginning of the new world that Israel's God had always intended to make. That is the first and perhaps the most important thing to know about the meaning of Easter."[2] Because the tomb is empty, the cosmos can experience restoration.

This is what explains the drastic change in the minds and attitudes of those early disciples turned apostles between the crucifixion of Jesus and the book of Acts: in the empty tomb, the plot of salvation found its resolution, the redemption of heaven and earth became possible. That Sunday morning was the disciples' D-Day.

---

1. Beale, *Teologia Bíblica*, 205.
2. N. T. Wright, *Simply Jesus*, 187.

The biblical message about our salvation should not be reduced to a sentimental doctrine, because it concerns an event. Christian faith is predicated on an empty tomb. Our security is as unshakable as the fact that "the living" one is no longer "among the dead." Jesus, the new Adam and our great Champion, defeated death and is Lord of all. Just as the resurrection transformed those perplexed disciples into martyrs, so it is intended to turn our own world upside down.

Part IV

From the Empty Tomb to the New Jerusalem

16

Worshipers from All the Nations: The Mission of the Messianic People

Now the eleven disciples went to Galilee, to the mountain to which Jesus had directed them. When they saw him, they worshiped him; but some doubted. And Jesus came and said to them, "All authority in heaven and on earth has been given to me. Go therefore and make disciples of all nations, baptizing them in the name of the Father and of the Son and of the Holy Spirit, and teaching them to obey everything that I have commanded you. And remember, I am with you always, to the end of the age." (Matthew 28:16–20)

Darrell Johnson used to start his courses on Christian Education at Regent College by telling the story of Smith Corona, a typewriter factory that enjoyed considerable market value up until the 1980s. The company was so successful that its products were often on the wish lists of regular middle-class Americans. The advent of the Internet within the following decade, however, was enough to sweep the Smith Coronas out of the stores. With the digital revolution, typewriters inevitably became obsolete. Given that the self-perception of the company was so deeply bound up with selling those machines, its sense of mission could not keep up with the rapidly changing culture of the 1990s, not to mention the speed of the new electronic devices.

Stanford researcher Jim Collins makes a similar observation, though not referring to the example of Smith Corona. Having examined a wide variety of leadership models, from West Point Academy to Bank of America, Collins notes that one of the key components differentiating "good" organizations from "great" ones is the ability to define the future primarily in terms of who to build it with.[1] In other words, the success of companies that grow strong across generations is usually directed not by the activity itself, but rather by people who are capable of doing two things: preserving the organization's core values on the one hand, and translating those values clearly through the many cultural transitions on the other hand.

We should be very careful in applying corporate principles to the church. In managing ecclesial communities as if they were companies, many Christians in Brazil have distanced themselves from the central values of God's kingdom and preached a false gospel (see the "health and wealth" megachurches, for example). My hesitation notwithstanding, this basic point seems valid for followers of the risen Christ: if our mission is defined primarily by our activities, as if we were to sell a product or a service, we quickly lose sight of our frame of reference and become irrelevant – even if we may enjoy momentary visibility.

To be sure, there are very many things that the church must in fact *do* in order to achieve its goals. But, as Johnson insists, the only way we can gauge our success is by reminding ourselves that there is a significant difference between "church work" and "the work of the church."[2] Whereas the former includes all activities related to the functioning of the local community – for instance, the maintenance of the building, the annual events, the Sunday bulletins, and so on – the latter is the true mission of Jesus's followers. And it is only when we pay attention to the hierarchy that exists between these two – "church work" should facilitate the execution of "the work of the church" – that we remain faithful to our task.

So what exactly is "the work of the church"? To begin with, it is important to stress that to be the church is also to receive a calling from God. The result of everything God accomplished throughout the biblical story is not merely a nice idea intended to make us feel better, nor is it merely the guarantee that we will "go to heaven" after we die. Yes, thank God, the gospel has implications for our eternal future, but this is not the whole picture. As we have previously noted, the Gospel of Matthew presents Jesus the Messiah as the climax of the story of salvation which God had begun in Genesis. He is the ideal descendant of David and of Abraham, the one who inaugurated the kingdom of God and recovered the human vocation, representing his people not only in his life but also in his death. Jesus's resurrection is in continuity with the Creator's desire

---

1. Collins, *Good to Great*, 41–45.
2. Johnson actually borrows from Richard Halverson on this point.

to see all the families of the earth being blessed through the offspring of the first patriarch, fully to dwell, in the end, in his cosmic temple.

Once we recall this Matthean emphasis, it is difficult to imagine how the first gospel could have ended if not by presenting the Great Commission. Given that the empty tomb confirms that death has been defeated, the risen Christ makes it clear to his followers that a new cosmic order has begun: "All authority in heaven and on earth has been given to me" (Matt 28:18). If chaos had exerted its tyranny since the fall of Adam and Eve, Christ now reigns through his victory over the grave. In the light of the resurrection, we must agree with Abraham Kuyper: "There is not a square inch in the whole domain of our human existence over which Christ, who is Sovereign over all, does not cry, Mine!"[3] All things in heaven and on earth are under the lordship of Jesus, God incarnate, who overcame the reality of Genesis 3.

It follows from this that the disciples of the Messiah are called to live out this reality, being the community in which his supreme authority is expressed in tangible ways. This is why, as soon as the risen Christ affirms his lordship, he gives a central command guiding all the activities with which the church should be preoccupied: "the work of the church" is to live the gospel – in allegiance to the King and according to the values of his kingdom[4] – and to call a people of worshipers from all the nations, in eschatological fulfillment of God's redemptive plan initiated in Abraham.

In more specific terms, the disciples are given the task to express Christ's lordship by making other disciples: "Go therefore and make disciples of all nations" (Matt 28:19). If Jesus himself saw that there was no other way to carry out the restoration of humanity – and the cosmos – except by calling people to follow him, the obvious conclusion is that "the work of the church" is to continue this project, by making other disciples of Jesus. Accordingly, there is nothing more important for the church than engaging and investing in discipleship. No matter how urgent (or perhaps attractive to our sensibilities) other activities may seem, if such things do not contribute to the most supreme calling of making followers of Jesus, we fall short of our raison d'être – even if our financial income, political influence, or exposure on social media makes us feel on top of the game.

---

3. Quoted in Bratt, *Abraham Kuyper*, 488.

4. For a detailed treatment of the theme of allegiance in the New Testament, see Matthew W. Bates, *Gospel Allegiance: What Faith in Jesus Misses for Salvation in Christ* (Grand Rapids: Brazos, 2019).

And how exactly does the risen Christ expect his people to achieve this goal? The Great Commission does not provide us with a method – Jesus never sends his disciples to photocopy a handout! – but instead outlines three fundamental principles, without which the mission of the church gets severely compromised. Whatever strategies life's circumstances force us to adopt, we can never neglect these points.

First, the scope of the messianic people's work is, by definition, multiethnic, "of all nations" (Matt 28:19). God did not call Abraham to make him someone important – the calling of Abraham was never ultimately about *Abraham*. By blessing the patriarchs, forming Israel, and resurrecting Jesus, God has always intended for his goodness to reach "all the families of the earth" (Gen 12:3). The last book of the Bible depicts the consummation of the kingdom as the gathering of "a great multitude that no one could count, from every nation, from all tribes and peoples and languages, standing before the throne and before the Lamb, robed in white, with palm branches in their hands" (Rev 7:9) – namely, a huge crowd corresponding to the totality of God's people, symbolically described by the number "one hundred forty-four thousand" in the previous passage (Rev 7:1–8). Jesus is Lord of the entire universe, and his salvation is intended for all the "four corners of the earth."

Second, because Jesus alone is Lord – and hence the only way to salvation – no other criterion warrants the gathering of disciples "of all nations," except the grace given by the Trinity in Christ. And this is publicly declared in the event of baptism: "baptizing them in the name of the Father and of the Son and of the Holy Spirit" (Matt 28:19). It is the task of the church, therefore, to affirm whoever trusts and follows Jesus as belonging to the community engendered by the Triune God. The people of the risen Christ are part of the new creation reconciled to the Father, through the Son, by the power of the Holy Spirit. There is not a single moment in the story of salvation suggesting that the gospel is about "me and God," to the surprise of many Western evangelicals. The focus has always been on the building up of a people, transformed according to the image of the Creator. (A sentimental cliché which, albeit corny and downright hollow, still holds sway among many Brazilian Christians is the idea that the believer does not need the community of faith. They insist that "I" am the church, so "I" don't have to *attend* the church. But the Bible never suggests that "I" am the church – and "you" are not the church either. "We" are the church – "we" who have been reached by the Trinity in Jesus and welcomed into the messianic people through baptism.)

And finally, the followers of the risen Christ are to devote themselves to Jesus's instructions: "and teaching them to obey everything that I have commanded you" (Matt 28:20). The mission of the church, in other words, is pedagogical. This, however, should not be understood as a kind of imperialistic proselytizing, nor merely as the imparting of propositional statements. Such a teaching goes far beyond the transfer of information; it focuses on *obedience* to the Messiah's ways: "teaching them to obey." The mission of the messianic people involves the transmission of the objective content of the gospel, but one can only learn to *obey* Jesus's instructions when these are visibly *embodied* by those proclaiming these truths. Simply put, only a disciple can be involved in discipling others. Discipleship can be possible, then, when the church lives out the lordship of the Messiah by modeling what it means to follow him in all aspects of life: in love for one another, in persistent prayer, in forgiveness of our debtors, in helping the vulnerable, in humble service, in hard work, in social justice, in care for creation – in everything that Jesus has taught. And, having come to fulfill "the law and the prophets," Jesus has taught his people very many things indeed! The risen Messiah is Lord over all.

That said, the Great Commission may strike us with a sense of inadequacy. After all, who can perfectly fulfill these tasks? And yet, Jesus knows his followers' limitations. He knows, much better than us, that we are incapable of accomplishing our mission on our own. For this reason, the Great Commission does not end with imperatives, but rather with a promise. The redemption of the cosmos and the restoration of humanity have always been God's work. And it is because this work belongs to the Creator alone that Jesus reminds his followers: the risen Christ himself will join together all the pieces of the puzzle. Accordingly, what guarantees the positive outcome of our mission is not our competence, or lack thereof, but the assurance that Jesus himself accompanies us in this endeavor, and will continue to do so until he returns to consummate his kingdom: "And remember, I am with you always, to the end of the age" (Matt 28:20). God has staked all his chips on this business, and nothing will be wasted in his hands.

17

Babel Reversed: The Presence of the Holy Spirit in the Church

When the day of Pentecost had come, they were all together in one place. And suddenly from heaven there came a sound like the rush of a violent wind, and it filled the entire house where they were sitting. Divided tongues, as of fire, appeared among them, and a tongue rested on each of them. All of them were filled with the Holy Spirit and began to speak in other languages, as the Spirit gave them ability.

Now there were devout Jews from every nation under heaven living in Jerusalem. And at this sound the crowd gathered and was bewildered, because each one heard them speaking in the native language of each. Amazed and astonished, they asked, "Are not all these who are speaking Galileans? And how is it that we hear, each of us, in our own native language? Parthians, Medes, Elamites, and residents of Mesopotamia, Judea and Cappadocia, Pontus and Asia, Phrygia and Pamphylia, Egypt and the parts of Libya belonging to Cyrene, and visitors from Rome, both Jews and proselytes, Cretans and Arabs – in our own languages we hear them speaking about God's deeds of power." All were amazed and perplexed, saying to one another, "What does this mean?" (Acts 2:1–12)

We simply cannot emphasize enough the central claim of the New Testament: the grand story of salvation finds its completion in Jesus Christ. Israel's Messiah and humanity's ultimate representative, the ideal descendant of David and of Abraham, entered the crossroads of human failure and God's intention to restore his cosmic temple, taking the biblical plot to its climax. Jesus defeated death and established the kingdom of God "on earth as it is in heaven": the "isolation" of God's image bearers from the Creator is finally overcome. So, before ascending to the right hand of the Father, the Son of God not only assures his disciples that he has "all authority in heaven and on earth" (Matt 28:18), but also gives them the nonnegotiable task to teach people "of all nations" to keep his ways (Matt 28:19).

At this point, however, we need to recall the fact that the disciples cannot accomplish their work by themselves. Indeed, throughout the Bible, the cause of almost every problem in the world has been the human tendency to do things our own way. Both the creation and the redemption of the cosmos were initiated and sustained by God alone. Accordingly, the mission of the church depends on God, and it is he who continues his work through those who follow Christ. No wonder the Great Commission ends with a promise: the presence of the one who conquered death will accompany his people to the end (Matt 28:20). The work of the church is to live out Jesus's reversal of Genesis 3.

Luke presents a similar emphasis. In the book of Acts, the evangelist tells us how the risen Christ continues his work through his followers. Aside from the peculiar interests of each author, we find a significant overlap between Matthew 28:16–20 and Acts 1:6–11:

> So when they had come together, they asked him, "Lord, is this the time when you will restore the kingdom to Israel?" He replied, "It is not for you to know the times or periods that the Father has set by his own authority. But you will receive power when the Holy Spirit has come upon you; and you will be my witnesses in Jerusalem, in all Judea and Samaria, and to the ends of the earth." When he had said this, as they were watching, he was lifted up, and a cloud took him out of their sight. While he was going and they were gazing up toward heaven, suddenly two men in white robes stood by them. They said, "Men of Galilee, why do you stand looking up toward heaven? This Jesus, who has been taken up from you into heaven, will come in the same way as you saw him go into heaven."

In short, the disciples are to proclaim the lordship of the risen Christ "in Jerusalem, in all Judea and Samaria, and to the ends of the earth." As the "two men in white robes" remind Peter and his friends, to belong to Jesus does not mean to stand "looking up toward heaven," but rather to participate in the kingdom already inaugurated by the Messiah, who "will come in the same way as you saw him go into heaven." But the crucial detail is that, until we are resurrected like Jesus, in one way or another we will still experience the reality of Genesis 3, with all the limitations that the present age imposes on us. So, given that the church can carry out its vocation only alongside the risen Christ, Luke insists on the centrality of the work of the Holy Spirit: "But you will receive power when the Holy Spirit has come upon you."

In order to understand what follows in the biblical plot, then, we must first note that Acts 2 is in full continuity with Jesus's empty tomb.[1] That is to say, the outpouring of God's presence happened precisely because the Messiah conquered death and assumed the highest position of authority in the universe. Peter's subsequent sermon makes this transparent: "This Jesus God raised up, and of that all of us are witnesses. Being therefore exalted at the right hand of God, and having received from the Father the promise of the Holy Spirit, he has poured out this that you both see and hear" (Acts 2:32–33). Since Jesus effectively addressed the rupture of Genesis 3, the Creator is now present among his people through his Spirit.

To speak of the work of Christ, therefore, necessarily leads us to speak of the gift of the Spirit. Any exposition of the gospel which does not include the outpouring of the divine presence on his people is as reductionistic as talking about Jesus without the cross. John the Baptist, in fact, had spoken of Jesus's ministry in connection with the hope for the coming of the Spirit: "I have baptized you with water; but he will baptize you with the Holy Spirit" (Mark 1:8 and parallels). The reality to which the temple has pointed in Israel's history – namely, the space wherein the Creator manifested his glory, in allusion to Eden – is now extended to Jesus's followers. In other words, the presence of the Holy Spirit in the community of the risen Christ is another confirmation of the redemption of the cosmos as God's dwelling place, a micro-representation of his temple restored. As Paul insists in Ephesians 2:17–22:

> So he came and proclaimed peace to you who were far off and peace to those who were near; for through him both of us have access in one Spirit to the Father. So then you are no longer strangers and aliens, but you are citizens with the saints and also members of the household of God, built upon the foundation of the apostles and prophets, with Christ Jesus himself as the cornerstone. In him the whole structure is joined together and grows into a holy temple in the Lord; in whom you also are built together spiritually into a dwelling place for God.

---

1. It is impossible to deal fully here with the theme of the Holy Spirit in the New Testament. See Fee, *God's Empowering Presence*; and Keener, *Spirit in the Gospels and Acts*.

Excursus: Jesus and the Temple in the Gospels

Given the centrality of the temple as YHWH's dwelling place throughout the Old Testament, a brief comment regarding Jesus's stance towards the Jerusalem temple is in order.

Since the influential work of E. P. Sanders,[2] it has been common ground among biblical scholars – especially those interested in the history behind the gospels – to regard Jesus's climactic actions at the temple (cf. Mark 11:15–17; Matt 21:12–13; Luke 19:45–46) as among the most important events of his life. This is a well-founded view, since Jesus's crucifixion follows straight from the accusations brought against him before the Sanhedrin, that he had threatened the integrity of the Jerusalem house of worship (cf. Mark 14:53–58; Matt 26:57–61).

This event, however, has a complicated history of interpretation, and a detailed exegesis of the relevant passages goes well beyond the scope of the present (non-technical) book. Suffice it to say that, while most scholars agree on the temple incident's representing Jesus's symbolic enactment of the impending destruction of the temple, there is still no consensus as to precisely what motivated the incident.[3]

My own take, which I have argued extensively elsewhere,[4] considers the evidence in Mark and suggests the following: Jesus rejected neither the temple nor the Levitical system as such (e.g. Mark 1:44; Matt 5:23, 35), but announced the destruction of the Jerusalem temple as the divine judgment on the priestly elite. According to Mark, Jesus the Messiah was the only one who could fulfill the vision of Isaiah 56:7 – to make the temple "a house of prayer for all peoples" – but the priests had obstinately rejected him. As a result, the Herodian temple would face God's wrath, just like the first temple in the days of Jeremiah. Hence the allusion to Jeremiah 7:11 in Mark 11:17.

What is most relevant for our present purposes, in any case, is that already in the gospels we see Jesus predict that the reality represented by the temple would soon be extended to the eschatological people of God, and Jesus himself would be the "cornerstone" of this people (cf. Mark 12:9–11; Matt 21:41–43). The temple language used by Paul in Ephesians 2:17–22 seems to be in continuity with this idea.

---

2. Sanders, *Jesus and Judaism*.

3. Cho, *Royal Messianism*, 3–16, 139–58.

4. Cho, 139–58.

According to Acts 2:1–12, moreover, the Spirit enables the people of God to fulfill their vocation. This is the significance of the disciples' speaking in "other languages" when filled with the presence of God. In the tenth chapter of this book, we saw that Joel depicts the final salvation of God's people in terms of the outpouring of the divine presence on everyone, regardless of status: "in the last days" the chosen people as a whole – not just those set apart for "special functions" – would be able to prophesy. When asked what the phenomenon of speaking in "other languages" could mean, Peter interprets Pentecost as the fulfillment of Joel's vision.

It is important to stress that these "other languages" were never meant to be an end in themselves. The mention of Judea among the regions from which the Jews had come to celebrate Pentecost in Jerusalem is relevant (Acts 2:9–11).[5] In the first century, the mother tongue of most Judeans was likely the very same as the language spoken in Galilee – namely, Aramaic. If the Jews from Judea heard some of those Galilean disciples speak in Aramaic, it means that the latter were simply talking in their mother tongue. The disciples spoke in "other languages" so that *all* could hear, in their "own languages," about "God's deeds of power" (2:11).[6] But, while some disciples spoke in other tongues, others did not. But *all* of them were filled with the power of the Holy Spirit, and thus *all* of them at that moment could witness to the greatness of the God revealed in Jesus. (In 1 Corinthians 14, Paul seems to presuppose the same logic, reminding the immature Christians of Corinth that "speaking in tongues" in a context where no one understands what is being said is useless for the building up of the body of Christ. The gifts of the Spirit are solely for the service of the church through the intelligible proclamation of the gospel, not for putting the spotlight on those endowed with supposedly special abilities.)

This is what Luke tells us in his account of the day of Pentecost: with Jesus's victory over the forces of chaos and the descent of the Holy Spirit on the community of the risen Christ, humanity's fragmentation began to be reversed. We thus see an important resolution of the confusion of Babel in

---

5. There is a slight textual problem here, to be sure, as a few (later, patristic) manuscripts attest the substitution of *Ioudaian* with other words. But this could be due to the fact that the naming of *Ioudaian* among foreign regions may have seemed odd to later scribes. Furthermore, the inhabitants of Judea spoke the same language as the Galilean disciples of Jesus – namely, Aramaic – and so the occurrence of *Ioudaian* may have appeared even stranger in the context of the "other languages." The evidence found in other (earlier) manuscripts, however, strongly favors the reading of *Ioudaian* in Acts 2:9. And, as I go on to point out, to note that some of the disciples spoke in their mother tongue (now empowered by the Spirit) seems to be precisely Luke's point in the passage.

6. This is the case even if one prefers the omission of *Ioudaian*.

Genesis 11:1–9, where humanity was scattered as a result of their autonomous desire to make a great name for themselves. In Christ and by the power of the Spirit, such dispersion is overcome: people from different places and cultures can now see God's wonderful deeds in the gospel. In this regard, it is suggestive that the call of Abraham immediately follows the account of the Tower of Babel, but it is only after the resurrection of Abraham's ideal descendant that God's glory reaches the nations.

The descent of the Holy Spirit in Acts 2 is therefore a "once and for all" event, not unlike the life, death, and resurrection of Jesus. This is not to say, of course, that it is unnecessary for the church to strive to be filled with the Holy Spirit – this happens in Acts 4:31, and Paul instructs his readers to do so in Ephesians 5:18–20. But Acts 2 is the fulfillment of Joel 2 and, as such, represents what happens to all those who are included thereafter in the community of the risen Lord. Again, Peter's sermon *after* the outpouring of the Spirit at Pentecost indicates precisely this: "Repent, and be baptized every one of you in the name of Jesus Christ so that your sins may be forgiven; and you will receive the gift of the Holy Spirit" (Acts 2:38). And this is true not only for Jews, but also for Gentiles. The eventual receiving of the Spirit by Samaritans as well as by Cornelius, a Roman centurion, which in many significant ways preludes Paul's gentile mission, demonstrates the universal scope of such a gift (Acts 8:4–25; 10:1–48).[7]

And how should the presence of the Holy Spirit be experienced after Pentecost, in the disciples' everyday lives? It is by no means incidental that, having reported all the spectacular things which happened to the disciples on that day, Luke gives us a very clear picture of the immediate result of God's dwelling among the church:

> They devoted themselves to the apostles' teaching and fellowship,
> to the breaking of bread and the prayers.

---

7. In Acts 8:4–25, it was necessary for the believers in Samaria to receive the Spirit through the Jerusalem leaders probably because of the long history of enmity between the Jews and the Samaritans. Peter's visit showed that the gift of the Spirit formed a single people, united in Christ. Later on, in Acts 10:1–48, the Spirit "falls" on Cornelius in a visible way, for this time it was necessary for Peter and his companions to understand that salvation was also for the Gentiles. Peter himself is depicted in Acts 11:15–18 as reporting: "'As I began to speak, the Holy Spirit fell upon them just as it had upon us at the beginning. And I remembered the word of the Lord, how he had said, "John baptized with water, but you will be baptized with the Holy Spirit." If then God gave them the same gift that he gave us when we believed in the Lord Jesus Christ, who was I that I could hinder God?' When they heard this, they were silenced. And they praised God, saying, 'Then God has given even to the Gentiles the repentance that leads to life'" (see also Acts 15:6–11). Acts 19:1–10, for its part, tells us that Paul needed to teach about the Spirit to some people in Ephesus, given that they had only heard about the baptism of John.

> Awe came upon everyone, because many wonders and signs were being done by the apostles. All who believed were together and had all things in common; they would sell their possessions and goods and distribute the proceeds to all, as any had need. Day by day, as they spent much time together in the temple, they broke bread at home and ate their food with glad and generous hearts, praising God and having the goodwill of all the people. And day by day the Lord added to their number those who were being saved. (Acts 2:42–47)

Simply put, the Spirit shapes a community of worshipers who live in the light of the lordship of Christ, reflecting his character in all their relationships. The new exodus actualized by the risen King produces a people who reflect the Creator's way of being. Filled with the Spirit himself, moreover, the earliest Christians are not led to gain influence among the powerful by force. At critical junctures in Acts, God takes the disciples to proclaim the resurrection to the elite, but the community which emerges from Pentecost fulfills its calling primarily by dedicating itself to discipleship – hence the focus on the "apostles' teaching," community life, the public celebration of the Eucharist, prayer, and faithful acts of service. And the one who makes the work of the church fruitful is God himself: "Day by day the Lord added to their number those who were being saved" (2:47; cf. 2:43).

It is hard not to feel a little uncomfortable when we compare Luke's portrayal of what it means to be filled with the power of God with the individualistic and consumerist standards that many evangelicals follow today, according to which numerical growth and political hegemony are the only things that matter. But, upon reflection, the community depicted in Acts 2:42–47, albeit unpretentious, is thoroughly counterintuitive. The reality of Genesis 3 has so deeply affected us that only God's own Spirit is able to generate a Christ-centered people. It is surely instructive that Luke tells us that those who came to believe through Peter's preaching "devoted themselves" to discipleship. The Greek verb *proskartereō* has the sense of "persisting" and connotes intentionality: they persevered in "the apostles' teaching and fellowship," in "the breaking of bread and the prayers." These practices constitute the core of our mission; whatever our strategies, we must never lose sight of them.

Global pandemics pose challenges for us all, so we have had to be creative in the past months in order to "persevere" in the practices which define us as the people of the risen Lord. And, by the grace of God, many opportunities have opened up for us to proclaim the resurrection of Jesus through new media. But being an active member of the church is not optional. To be saved is to be included in the community wherein God dwells through his Spirit so as to remake us in the image of the Son of God. In devoting ourselves to the realities which shape us into a Christ-centered people – namely, faithful biblical teaching, fellowship around the Lord's table, prayer, and concrete acts of service – we are being transformed by the divine presence and are participating in God's work of making his name known to the nations.

18

No Longer Condemned: The Spirit of Adoption

There is therefore now no condemnation for those who are in Christ Jesus. For the law of the Spirit of life in Christ Jesus has set you free from the law of sin and of death. For God has done what the law, weakened by the flesh, could not do: by sending his own Son in the likeness of sinful flesh, and to deal with sin, he condemned sin in the flesh, so that the just requirement of the law might be fulfilled in us, who walk not according to the flesh but according to the Spirit. For those who live according to the flesh set their minds on the things of the flesh, but those who live according to the Spirit set their minds on the things of the Spirit. To set the mind on the flesh is death, but to set the mind on the Spirit is life and peace. For this reason the mind that is set on the flesh is hostile to God; it does not submit to God's law – indeed it cannot, and those who are in the flesh cannot please God.

But you are not in the flesh; you are in the Spirit, since the Spirit of God dwells in you. Anyone who does not have the Spirit of Christ does not belong to him. But if Christ is in you, though the body is dead because of sin, the Spirit is life because of righteousness. If the Spirit of him who raised Jesus from the dead dwells in you, he who raised Christ from the dead will give life to your mortal bodies also through his Spirit that dwells in you. (Rom 8:1–11)

One of the few advantages of having to stay home during the pandemic was that one ended up having more time than usual to catch up on movies and television shows. When I started drafting the sermon which would eventually become the source material for this chapter, I had just begun to watch *The Spy*, a drama series directed by Israeli filmmaker Gideon Raff and starring British actor Sacha Baron Cohen. The story is based on real events which happened to Eli Cohen, a Mossad agent who, under the alias Kamel Thaabet, infiltrated the high ranks of the Syrian government in the 1960s. Cohen is best known for relaying key information to the Israeli authorities regarding the Golan Heights during the Six-Day War, but it was one particular detail in Raff's characterization of Cohen that caught my attention.

In the opening scene of the first episode, Cohen finds himself in a prison in Syria, recently caught by the Damascus authorities and ready to sign a letter addressed to his wife, Nadia. But as he is about to finish the letter, Cohen hesitates, unsure which name to use with reference to himself – whether Eli or Kamel. The story then unfolds in retrospect, highlighting this internal struggle that the spy had to face over his identity during the years of service to the Mossad in Syria. On one occasion, when Cohen was visiting his homeland in order to plan the next stages of his mission, he felt so uncomfortable with ordinary life in Tel Aviv that he decided to hasten his return to Damascus. Despite seeing the economic and emotional hardships his family was going through due to his absence, he chose to return to Syria sooner than planned. Having lived in Kamel Thaabet's shoes for so long, Eli Cohen embraced an identity that had not originally belonged to him, and his decisions were influenced by a blurred perception of who he actually was.

As we have noted thus far, the reality of Genesis 3 placed all of us under the power of death, and the plot of God's salvation finds its turning point in Christ, the one who defeated death itself. The New Testament, however, describes the consequences of sin also in terms of condemnation. Just as no one can overcome the problem of Genesis 3 simply by willpower, it is impossible for sinners to be regarded as righteous by their own merit. The question we must address here concerns the implications of the work of Christ and the outpouring of the Holy Spirit for the damning effects of our transgressions. And the most appropriate text to look at in this regard is found in Romans.

Among other reasons, Paul wrote his letter to the Romans in preparation for his preaching ministry in Spain (Rom 15:22–29). But since he had never had the opportunity to visit the church in Rome before, Paul also took the opportunity to present the message he preached, highlighting some communal implications of the gospel for how Jews and Gentiles were together to live out their faith in Christ. This is why Romans is the letter in which Paul most painstakingly deals with the relation between God's gift in Christ and the meaning of Torah and circumcision.[1] What we find in this epistle is a very detailed exposition of how the gospel alone can bring about the sinner's salvation and inclusion into the eschatological people of God.

This central idea becomes clear in Romans 3. Having argued that humanity in general and the Jews in particular have fallen short of the "glory" of God, being subject to his "wrath" (Rom 1:18 – 3:8), Paul stresses Torah's inability to justify the sinner: "we have already charged that all, both Jews and Greeks, are under the power of sin. . . . For 'no human being will be justified in his sight' by deeds prescribed by the law, for through the law comes the knowledge of sin" (3:9, 20). As Paul insists in Romans 3:21–26, Jesus's blood is the only means by which one can have access to the divine presence and belong to the covenant community:

> But now, apart from law, the righteousness of God has been disclosed, and is attested by the law and the prophets, the righteousness of God through faith in Jesus Christ for all who believe. For there is no distinction, since all have sinned and fall short of the glory of God; they are now justified by his grace as a gift, through the redemption that is in Christ Jesus, whom God put forward as a sacrifice of atonement by his blood, effective through faith. He did this to show his righteousness, because in his divine forbearance he had passed over the sins previously committed; it was to prove at the present time that he himself is righteous and that he justifies the one who has faith in Jesus.

This is a complex passage, fraught with syntactic ambiguities which have generated heated scholarly debates, but suffice it to note a few (less controversial) points here.

First, while in Christ the sinner is declared righteous "apart from law," this is at the same time "attested by the law and the prophets." The gospel, in other words, is not opposed to what God had revealed throughout Israel's history, but rather is the very fulfillment of the plot of salvation (cf. Matt 5:17–20). Torah and the prophets pointed to a greater reality, a reality which Christ fully embodied.

Second, Paul alludes to the Day of Atonement, when the high priest was expected every year to sprinkle the blood of an animal on top of the ark of

---

1. See details in Moo, *Romans*, 16–22; and the seventh chapter in Barclay, *Paul and the Power of Grace*, titled "The Incongruous Gift and Its Fitting Results (Romans 1–5)" (Kindle loc. 1817–2099).

the covenant, also known as the "mercy seat," whence God would extend his forgiveness towards his people (see Lev 16:1–34).[2] Paul identifies Christ with the blood of the sacrificial victim that would be presented on those annual occasions (Lev 16:14–15) – "by his blood" (*en tǭautou haimati*). The point of this rich imagery is to affirm that, in his death on the cross, Christ fulfilled the reality foreshadowed in Leviticus 16:1–34, with the result that his blood atones definitively for the sins of his people and represents the means by which God pronounces his forgiveness over the sinner. God thus was consistent with regards both to his righteousness and to his desire to restore for himself a people: "it was to prove at the present time that he himself is righteous and that he justifies the one who has faith in Jesus" (Rom 3:26).

This could happen, moreover, only because God took the initiative: "by his grace as a gift." The Greek *dōrean tę̄ autou chariti* actually preserves an eloquent redundancy so as to emphasize the justification of the sinner as taking place *only* by God's unmerited favor. In Christ, God was faithful to his own character – "full of grace and truth" (cf. Exod 34:6) – not allowing our condemnation to be the end of the story. Given that all of us have failed to live in accordance with God's glory, therefore, our acquittal is possible only through the sufficient merit of Jesus, in whom we must place our exclusive trust: "they are now justified by his grace as a gift, through the redemption that is in Christ Jesus, whom God put forward as a sacrifice of atonement by his blood, effective through faith" (Rom 3:24–25a).

But the fact that we are declared to stand in right relationship both with God and with his people through the work of Christ alone is not the whole story. In fact, in the verse that serves as a programmatic summary for the entire letter, the apostle affirms the gospel as "the power of God for salvation" (1:16). Accordingly, the implications of Christ's work for us are not only forensic, so to speak, but also transformative. The gospel is the *power* of God that saves the sinner. So, while many Christians still insist on interpreting Romans solely through the lens of Romans 3:21–26, there is much more to be said about Paul's exposition of the gospel in this letter. In Romans 5:1–11, for example, Paul explains that our justification in Christ results in reconciliation with God and the assurance that his everlasting love has been bestowed upon us through the Holy Spirit: "Therefore, since we are justified by faith, we have peace with God

---

2. The Greek term translated as "sacrifice of atonement" in Rom 3:25 is *hilastērion*, which in the Greek version of Lev 16:2 refers to the mercy seat. The NRSV suggests that *hilastērion* is connected to the sin offering, but the evidence indicates otherwise. In the Septuagint, the expression more commonly used with reference to the sin offering is *peri hamartias*, which Paul deploys in Rom 8:3 to speak of Jesus's dealing with sin in his flesh.

through our Lord Jesus Christ. . . . God's love has been poured into our hearts through the Holy Spirit that has been given to us" (5:1, 5). And the pinnacle of Paul's argument is found in Romans 8, where we see how "the power of God for salvation" acts upon those who trust in Jesus.

It is important to realize, then, that Romans 8 is the climax of everything Paul has been talking about since the beginning of the epistle: "There is therefore now no condemnation for those who are in Christ Jesus" (8:1). The conjunction "therefore" connects the statement with the things the apostle just said in the previous paragraph, but the exclamation in the verse immediately preceding Romans 8:1 – "Thanks be to God through Jesus Christ our Lord!" (7:25) – is in full continuity with the first parts of the letter. In short, a crucial outcome of Jesus's resurrection is that the inexorable burden of guilt resulting from human autonomy is removed from the shoulders of those who trust in Jesus. And Paul justifies this claim in Romans 8:3–4 by expanding on what he had explained in Romans 3:21–26: there is no condemnation for those who are in Christ because Christ fulfilled the human vocation – "he condemned sin in the flesh" (8:3) – thus breaking the very power of sin through his death.

A well-known analogy for the effect of God's gift in Christ is that we had a billion-dollar debt in the bank, only to find out one day that said debt was forgiven – not because the bank decided to "delete" our negative balance from the system, but because the owner of the bank actually took it out of his own pocket to pay what we owed. Or, to be consistent with the language we have been using throughout this book, we were all sentenced to eternal death as a result of Genesis 3, but Jesus has overcome our death through his own crucifixion. Putting the emphasis on the fact that God did not merely "ignore" our condemnation, but actually paid for it, makes all the difference: our sentence has effectively been served; it no longer exists. The guilt of our sins is not something which has been merely set aside for a moment; it has been torn apart. God made himself our representative and solved our death.

However, the real thrust of Romans 8 – and the wonder of the gospel – is that, in Christ, God not only delivers us from the *penalty* of death, but also dwells with us. This coheres with the point we made in the previous chapter: Jesus rose from the dead and poured out the Holy Spirit on his people (Acts 2:1–13). In the rest of Romans 8, therefore, the apostle insists that the gospel entails much more than the "substitutionary" role Jesus played on our behalf, asserting that our salvation is actualized through the very presence of the Spirit among the community of believers: "For the law of the Spirit of life in Christ Jesus has set you free from the law of sin and of death" (8:2). It is precisely in this way that the gospel is the power of God in action to save all those who believe: in Christ, God not only justifies us and reconciles us to himself, but also transforms us by the power that raised Jesus from the dead. "You are in the Spirit, since the Spirit of God dwells in you. . . . If the Spirit of him who raised Jesus from the dead dwells in you, he who raised Christ from the dead will give life to your mortal bodies also through his Spirit that dwells in you" (8:9, 11). What splendid news! Our justification by faith is just the beginning of what it means to be saved. We are declared righteous in Christ so that we may enjoy peace with God today and be restored in the likeness of our King until our final resurrection from the dead at the consummation of the ages. We all experience death in the likeness of Adam, but we will experience resurrection in the likeness of Christ (5:12–21).

And there is more: by accomplishing these things for us in Christ, God changes our identity. We are no longer descendants of Adam and slaves of sin; we are children of God and heirs of eternal life with Christ. In Christ, the Supreme Judge of the cosmos declares us righteous, invites us to fellowship with him, and now includes us in his family, making us inheritors of all his riches. And here we must not fail to see the parallels with the prerogatives belonging to Abraham's descendants, which are now extended to anyone who trusts in Jesus (see also Eph 2). This explains why, at this high point in his exposition of the gospel, Paul speaks of the end result of Christ's work using the language of adoption and inheritance of a new creation:

> So then, brothers and sisters, we are debtors, not to the flesh, to live according to the flesh – for if you live according to the flesh, you will die; but if by the Spirit you put to death the deeds of the body, you will live. For all who are led by the Spirit of God are children of God. For you did not receive a spirit of slavery to fall back into fear, but you have received a spirit of adoption. When we cry, "Abba! Father!" it is that very Spirit bearing witness with our spirit that we are children of God, and if children, then heirs, heirs of God and joint heirs with Christ – if, in fact, we suffer with him so that we may also be glorified with him. (Rom 8:12–17)

Right now, God is not thinking of destroying us, nor is he waiting for the moment we stumble in order to chastise us. In Christ, we are adopted by the Creator of the cosmos, the same God who throughout the centuries has revealed himself as absolutely good, patient, and faithful to his promises. True, YHWH never yields to our sinful inclinations, and every stubbornness in following fallen standards of "good and evil" will result in chaos and death. Nevertheless, though we still make mistakes, God desires our flourishing and transforms us into the image of Jesus. The loving Father of our Lord Jesus Christ has made us members of his family. He does not hate us; he loves us. This is what defines our identity. The present age and some of our old habits may suggest otherwise, but that's because the world surrounding us remains, to some significant degree, deeply out of place. Be that as it may, the gospel has already changed our identity, the gospel has given us a new name. And what is secured for us is resurrection – eternal life with God at the consummation of the new creation.

This means that our experience in this post-Genesis 3 world in no way contradicts the reality of our adoption by God. In fact, it is precisely in the broken context wherein we still find ourselves that the gospel really is seen as the power of God for our salvation. In Romans 8:18–27, Paul states that the same Spirit who raised Jesus from the dead and now dwells among us sustains us on our journey to the end:

> I consider that the sufferings of this present time are not worth comparing with the glory about to be revealed to us. For the creation waits with eager longing for the revealing of the children of God; for the creation was subjected to futility, not of its own will but by the will of the one who subjected it, in hope that the creation itself will be set free from its bondage to decay and will obtain the freedom of the glory of the children of God. We know that the whole creation has been groaning in labor pains until now; and not only the creation, but we ourselves, who have the first fruits of the Spirit, groan inwardly while we wait for adoption, the redemption of our bodies. For in hope we were saved. Now hope that is seen is not hope. For who hopes for what is seen? But if we hope for what we do not see, we wait for it with patience.
>
> Likewise the Spirit helps us in our weakness; for we do not know how to pray as we ought, but that very Spirit intercedes with sighs too deep for words. And God, who searches the heart, knows what is the mind of the Spirit, because the Spirit intercedes for the saints according to the will of God.

Given that the kingdom we will inherit with Christ is characterized by his cruciform glory, not even the sufferings we go through in life are wasted in God's hands as a means of shaping our character. Creation itself "groans" in anticipation of the restoration of humanity, awaiting its emancipation from the "decay" to which it was subjected because of sin. Far from shielding us from pain or giving us an escapist hope, then, the Spirit adjusts our perspective according to what God has already accomplished at Jesus's first coming, so that life's many hurdles contribute to our maturity as disciples. This is what we call sanctification.

Furthermore, the Spirit also helps us in what is most essential for our journey as the people of God, by teaching us to pray. The Spirit teaches us how to pray in different situations in life as well as interceding for us when we do not know how to pray. Even in what is most fundamental to our relationship with God, he himself helps us through his Spirit. The gospel really is good news: "We know that all things work together for good for those who love God, who are called according to his purpose" (8:28).

In the light of this, the Christian life must be understood as the life in the Spirit. Since our identity is defined by the adoption we have received in Christ, the plot of salvation invites us to become, by the power of the Spirit, what we already are in Christ.[3] The power of the one who raised Jesus from the dead broke the hold that sin had on us (6:1 – 7:6), placing us under the lordship of Christ. We are subjects of the risen Christ, called to be "led by the Spirit of God," walking according to the truth of the gospel and preoccupying ourselves with all the things that God has accomplished for us in Christ. And until our final resurrection happens, we may join Paul in confidently declaring that nothing can separate us from God's love:

> What then are we to say about these things? If God is for us, who is against us? He who did not withhold his own Son, but gave him up for all of us, will he not with him also give us everything else? Who will bring any charge against God's elect? It is God who justifies. Who is to condemn? It is Christ Jesus, who died, yes, who was raised, who is at the right hand of God, who indeed intercedes for us. Who will separate us from the love of Christ? Will hardship, or distress, or persecution, or famine, or nakedness, or peril, or sword? As it is written,
>
> "For your sake we are being killed all day long;
>   we are accounted as sheep to be slaughtered."
>
> No, in all these things we are more than conquerors through him who loved us. For I am convinced that neither death, nor life, nor angels, nor rulers, nor things present, nor things to come, nor powers, nor height, nor depth, nor anything else in all creation, will be able to separate us from the love of God in Christ Jesus our Lord. (Rom 8:31–39)

---

3. Moo, *Romans*, 391.

19

Samples of an Alternative World: The People of Reconciliation

> I have heard of your faith in the Lord Jesus and your love toward all the saints, and for this reason I do not cease to give thanks for you as I remember you in my prayers. I pray that the God of our Lord Jesus Christ, the Father of glory, may give you a spirit of wisdom and revelation as you come to know him, so that, with the eyes of your heart enlightened, you may know what is the hope to which he has called you, what are the riches of his glorious inheritance among the saints, and what is the immeasurable greatness of his power for us who believe, according to the working of his great power. God put this power to work in Christ when he raised him from the dead and seated him at his right hand in the heavenly places, far above all rule and authority and power and dominion, and above every name that is named, not only in this age but also in the age to come. And he has put all things under his feet and has made him the head over all things for the church, which is his body, the fullness of him who fills all in all. (Eph 1:15–23)

The year 2020 has been hands down the most challenging period since I became a pastor. In addition to the anxieties relating to COVID-19 – not only the risks of contracting the disease itself, but also its many political, social, and economic consequences – I cannot remember having to put so much effort into mending relationships which were broken simply due to differences in opinion. As I was writing the first draft of this chapter, two longtime friends from Brazil, who also happen to be church ministers, were publicly offending each other over the United States presidential elections.

(Some Brazilian Christians think it's their holy duty to import the cultural wars from North America to the southern tropics.) A few days later, I had to counsel a member of my church whose parents would not talk to him unless he took a stance against the safety protocols recommended by the World Health Organization and refused to wear masks.

Philosopher Byung-Chul Han acutely points out that distrust has become the norm in almost all spheres of contemporary society, and that social media has played a major role in crystalizing such a pattern of thought.[1] In a strange world where the (ill-informed) views of any inhabitant of the planet can go "viral," fake news and conspiracy theories abound, setting the tone for almost every conversation around the table. Our virtual engagements have rendered our actual relationships unstable. And the worst result of this phenomenon is that, in typically Orwellian fashion, people are constantly framing reality within strictly binary categories. If you do not hold the exact same opinions as I do, you are necessarily evil and therefore my enemy.

Even though the Messiah has already conquered death, the world remains profoundly disoriented. And, sadly, many Christians are to blame for the perpetuation of such a problem. But, according to the biblical story, the current culture of distrust is far from novel, probably representing the most immediate outcome of Genesis 3. At a fundamental level, that is, the chaos occasioned by human autonomy produced precisely the things we have just mentioned: alienation and enmity. In the third chapter, we saw that the episode following the expulsion of Adam and Eve from Eden is the murder of Abel by his own brother. Does the gospel have anything to say about this state of affairs? How do Jesus's resurrection and the presence of the Holy Spirit within the church help us to navigate the atmosphere of segregation so thick and pervasive around the globe since sin entered the world?

Paul's letter to the Ephesians is relevant to this matter, for in it the apostle explains what it means to be the people of the risen Christ.[2] It is instructive, though, that even before discussing the practical things the church is called to do, Paul devotes a significant amount of space – roughly the first half of the letter – to explaining what *God* has first accomplished in Jesus. This is no mere cosmetic exercise: the imperatives of Christian ethics are consistent with the integrity of the gospel only inasmuch as they are rooted in the indicatives of what Jesus actualized, not vice versa.

---

1. Han, *Transparency Society*.
2. Lincoln, *Ephesians*, xciii–xcv.

In the early parts of Ephesians Paul seems to presuppose much of what we have covered in the previous chapters of this book. In Ephesians 1:3–11, we read that Christ redeemed us through his blood, gave us the gift of adoption, gathered up all things under his lordship, and guaranteed our eternal inheritance:

> Blessed be the God and Father of our Lord Jesus Christ, who has blessed us in Christ with every spiritual blessing in the heavenly places, just as he chose us in Christ before the foundation of the world to be holy and blameless before him in love. He destined us for adoption as his children through Jesus Christ, according to the good pleasure of his will, to the praise of his glorious grace that he freely bestowed on us in the Beloved. In him we have redemption through his blood, the forgiveness of our trespasses, according to the riches of his grace that he lavished on us. With all wisdom and insight he has made known to us the mystery of his will, according to his good pleasure that he set forth in Christ, as a plan for the fullness of time, to gather up all things in him, things in heaven and things on earth. In Christ we have also obtained an inheritance, having been destined according to the purpose of him who accomplishes all things according to his counsel and will.

Additionally, in Ephesians 2:1–10, Paul reminds his readers that God granted humanity all these things by his mercy and love, while we were totally unable to regenerate ourselves:

> You were dead through the trespasses and sins in which you once lived, following the course of this world, following the ruler of the power of the air, the spirit that is now at work among those who are disobedient. All of us once lived among them in the passions of our flesh, following the desires of flesh and senses, and we were by nature children of wrath, like everyone else. But God, who is rich in mercy, out of the great love with which he loved us even when we were dead through our trespasses, made us alive together with Christ – by grace you have been saved – and raised us up with him and seated us with him in the heavenly places in Christ Jesus, so that in the ages to come he might show the immeasurable riches of his grace in kindness toward us in Christ Jesus. For by grace you been saved through faith, and this is not your own doing; it is the gift of God – not the result of works, so that no one may

boast. For we are what he has made us, created in Christ Jesus for good works, which God prepared beforehand to be our way of life.

What is worth highlighting here is this: since we are saved "by grace . . . through faith," there is no room in the gospel for human arrogance or elitism. The inescapable consequence of the gift we receive from God in Christ is the absolute rejection of boasting – "so that no one may boast." Faith, after all, is the antithesis of any human attempt at asserting merit before God. Accordingly, as John Barclay notes, God's undeserved grace manifested in Christ relativizes whatever system of values previously defined us as individuals.[3] In other words, what characterizes a true disciple of Jesus is the awareness that only God's unmerited favor extended through the life, death, and resurrection of Jesus can have ultimate claim on our identity. Ethnicity, lineage, family tradition, social status, economic power, education, gender, political opinion – however dearly these things may have been held by us when we lived "in the passions of our flesh, following the desires of flesh and senses," they can no longer determine who we are.

So, given that salvation is entirely by God's grace, what is dealt with at the cross is not only our problem with God, but also – and in equal measure – the animosity among humanity. A gospel that reconciles "me" with God without engendering peace within the community of faith is not the "power of God," but a product that soothes my narcissistic conscience. Jesus had taught something similar in the Sermon on the Mount: "So when you are offering your gift at the altar, if you remember that your brother or sister has something against you, leave your gift there before the altar and go; first be reconciled to your brother or sister, and then come and offer your gift" (Matt 5:23–24). And the way Paul chooses to underscore this truth in Ephesians 2:11–22 could not be more radical:

> So then, remember that at one time you Gentiles by birth, called "the uncircumcision" by those who are called "the circumcision" – a physical circumcision made in the flesh by human hands – remember that you were at that time without Christ, being aliens from the commonwealth of Israel, and strangers to the covenants of promise, having no hope and without God in the world. But now in Christ Jesus you who once were far off have been brought near by the blood of Christ. For he is our peace; in his flesh he

---

3. Throughout his recent book *Paul and the Power of Grace*, Barclay argues for a definition of "God's grace in Christ" in Paul's writings as "God's incongruous gift in Christ."

has made both groups into one and has broken down the dividing wall, that is, the hostility between us. He has abolished the law with its commandments and ordinances, that he might create in himself one new humanity in place of the two, thus making peace, and might reconcile both groups to God in one body through the cross, thus putting to death that hostility through it. So he came and proclaimed peace to you who were far off and peace to those who were near; for through him both of us have access in one Spirit to the Father. So then you are no longer strangers and aliens, but you are citizens with the saints and also members of the household of God, built upon the foundation of the apostles and prophets, with Christ Jesus himself as the cornerstone. In him the whole structure is joined together and grows into a holy temple in the Lord; in whom you also are built together spiritually into a dwelling place for God.

In Christ, uncircumcised Gentiles, who were previously foreign to the covenant, are now included in the people among whom the divine presence dwells, as members of his family and co-citizens of his kingdom. And lest the reader forget: if you are not a Jewish believer, you are counted among those "far off" to whom "peace" was "proclaimed." Paul's words find deep resonance in Peter's declaration at the Jerusalem Council in Acts 15:8–9: "God, who knows the human heart, testified to them [Gentiles] by giving them the Holy Spirit, just as he did to us; and in cleansing their hearts by faith he has made no distinction between them and us." The lordship of Jesus over heaven and earth, therefore, not only entails the destruction of the wall which separated the nations from God, but also responds to the alienation and enmity that have so characterized human relationships ever since Genesis 3. Christ reconciled us with the Father so that we may be a people primarily defined by his grace (Eph 2:14–15).

The question, then, concerns how the disciples of Jesus are to respond to the tensions existing in the world. Are we to "impose" the peace of the gospel on those around us? Should we encourage the leaders of the world's major religions to sing together *We Are the World* and to pretend to be best friends forever? Would our problems be gone the moment liberals and conservatives within the political spectrum started promoting a secular ecumenism of sorts?[4]

---

4. Behind these obviously naive suggestions, there is the crucial problem of how to define justice. On this, see Sandel, *Justice*, 305–23.

Paul proposes a more realistic way forward: it is the church – the people of the risen Christ, the new humanity shaped by God's undeserved grace – that is the space wherein the gospel of reconciliation is to become visible. This is obviously not to say that we can shy away from striving for peace outside our local communities. Christians should be models of peacemaking in all corners of society. Jesus himself taught, "Blessed are the peacemakers, for they will be called children of God" (Matt 5:9). The point, however, is that the most effective way of doing this outside the church is by example, by living out what it's like to be reconciled to God and to one another. As Lesslie Newbigin famously argued, a pluralistic society will be able to see the plausibility of the message of the cross only when the church embodies it.[5]

By contrast, when anything but the gospel occupies the center of our self-awareness – whether race, money, class, education, or political position – we despise Christ's work, forfeit our ultimate vocation, and worsen the fragmentation of the world. Simply put, we risk falling into idolatry. In a piece also written during the pandemic, Timothy Keller laments the growing tendency among American Christians to feel more comfortable among people supporting the same political party than among members of their own local churches.[6] I honestly thought Keller was describing the situation in Brazil, where prominent church leaders and theologians have systematically (and publicly) condemned to hell anyone not supporting their candidate. But if we say that we stand or fall solely on Christ's merit and because God chose "to make us alive" by his Spirit, it means that we have no right to determine who has access to the Lord's table based on social status, ethnicity, political opinion, or anything else that is not the gospel. When we build up the walls of enmity within the community of faith, we despise Christ's lordship and empty his cross. Think about this: Paul, who according to himself was the most exemplary Pharisee of his generation (Phil 3:4–6), says that not even circumcision matters in determining one's participation in the eschatological people of God: "For in Christ Jesus neither circumcision nor uncircumcision counts for anything; the only thing that counts is faith working through love" (Gal 5:6)!

We thus discover that God's salvation addresses head-on the spirit of estrangement so prevalent in our time, by reminding us that the disciples of Jesus are the Creator's answer to the fragmentation of the world. Later on in Ephesians, Paul states that God did all this "so that through the church the wisdom of God in its rich variety might now be made known to the rulers and

---

5. Newbigin, *Gospel in a Pluralist Society*, 228–29.
6. Keller, "Justice in the Bible."

authorities in the heavenly places" (Eph 3:10). Whenever different people – from different social backgrounds, ethnicities, and political preferences – gather together to sing praises, listen to the preaching of the Word, participate in the Lord's table, and declare peace to one another in fellowship, they are subverting the world's mindset, providing hard proof that Jesus began to reverse the alienating effects of death. The church is the divine manifesto that, in Christ, humanity and the cosmos are being restored.

Some people still assume that Christianity turned the Roman Empire upside down by imposing its dogmas on society or taking over places of power by force. In his classic work *The Rise of Christianity*, however, sociologist Rodney Stark demonstrates one important factor in the "success" of the early church: they welcomed society's most vulnerable into the Christian fellowship and cared for them as members of the same family.[7] Fourth-century Roman Emperor Julian is an important witness to this: "The impious Galileans support not only their poor, but ours as well, everyone can see that our people lack aid from us" (*Ep.* 22, 430C–D).[8] Further, worship in the early church took place around the table, where no distinction between Jew and Gentile, slave and free, rich and poor, educated and uneducated, was supposed to take place. (The Christians in Corinth seem to have forgotten this, as the rich among them were refusing to wait for the poor before starting the public worship, hence Paul's rebuke in 1 Cor 11:17–34.) So people from different backgrounds would sit next to one another, listen to the Eucharistic words of Jesus – "This is the body of Christ broken for you; this is the blood of Christ shed for your sins" – and together celebrate Christ's sacrificial gift. This showed the world that Jesus had indeed started a different way of being.

This is why, in Ephesians 4:1–6, Paul begins to explain the imperatives of the gospel by emphasizing the *unity* of the church:

> I therefore, the prisoner in the Lord, beg you to lead a life worthy of the calling to which you have been called, with all humility and gentleness, with patience, bearing with one another in love, making every effort to maintain the unity of the Spirit in the bond of peace. There is one body and one Spirit, just as you were called to the one hope of your calling, one Lord, one faith, one baptism, one God and Father of all, who is above all and through all and in all.

---

7. Stark, *Rise of Christianity*, 73–94.
8. Cited in Stark, 83–4.

Paul's words contradict almost everything that is encouraged in our culture today: instead of distrust and polarization, humility, kindness, and patient forbearance in love. This is the "calling" (*klēsis*) we have received in the gospel; this is our human vocation in Christ. All things in heaven and on earth were placed under Christ's authority, so that an "alternative society" could come into being, wherein God's cruciform character shapes our relations.

And it is important to emphasize that such a "unity of the Spirit in the bond of peace" is possible only insofar as we give up sentimental ideals and truly base our fellowship in the gift of Christ. As Dietrich Bonhoeffer has warned us, "Those who love their dream of a Christian community more than the Christian community itself become destroyers of that Christian community even though their personal intentions may be ever so honest, earnest, and sacrificial."[9] Indeed, for Paul, the unity of the church is predicated exclusively on the unity of the gospel: one body, one Spirit, one hope, one Lord, one faith, one baptism, and one God. In other words, there can be no unity in the church apart from faithfulness to the message of the cross.

In sum, the answer Christians must give these days, when even families are divided over what is reported in the news, is simply to be church: to worship God and exemplify the new humanity in Christ. The church is called to demonstrate beauty. Let us then live "to the praise of his glorious grace that he freely bestowed on us in the Beloved" (Eph 1:6), being the people of reconciliation.

---

9. Bonhoeffer, *Life Together*, 10.

20

In the End, God Will Dwell in the New Jerusalem: The Christian Hope

Then I saw a new heaven and a new earth; for the first heaven and the first earth had passed away, and the sea was no more. And I saw the holy city, the new Jerusalem, coming down out of heaven from God, prepared as a bride adorned for her husband. And I heard a loud voice from the throne saying,

> "See, the home of God is among mortals.
> He will dwell with them;
> they will be his peoples,
> and God himself will be with them;
> he will wipe every tear from their eyes.
> Death will be no more;
> mourning and crying and pain will be no more,
> for the first things have passed away." . . .

I saw no temple in the city, for its temple is the Lord God the Almighty and the Lamb. And the city has no need of sun or moon to shine on it, for the glory of God is its light, and its lamp is the Lamb. The nations will walk by its light, and the kings of the earth will bring their glory into it. Its gates will never be shut by day – and there will be no night there. People will bring into it the glory and the honor of the nations. (Rev 21:1–4, 22–26)

O ver the past few months, I have often wondered what life will be like when this book is finally published. Will the pandemic have become part of a distant memory? Will we have resumed all the in-person activities both at my home church and at the seminary where I teach in São Paulo? Will the small entrepreneurs I know have managed to get out of this grueling crisis? And how will the less privileged of my country survive the side effects of so many long weeks of lockdown? I suspect that, even if we return to some degree of normality in the near future, for a long time we will wrestle with a deep sense of disorientation. Few would disagree that the best word to describe life in recent months is "uncertainty." And uncertainty is what we will have to live with for a while.

But many of the disruptions caused by the coronavirus say more about us than about the circumstances themselves. On a basic level, COVID-19 has simply reminded us of a fact which we had conveniently suppressed in our minds: no one has ultimate control over the future. It is actually revealing that we were caught totally off guard. Many of us had fooled ourselves into thinking that our resources could guarantee a life without any problems, in resemblance to the rich man in the parable of Luke 12, who despite the apparent security of his wealth had to face God's warning: "You fool! This very night your life is being demanded of you. And the things you have prepared, whose will they be?" (Luke 12:20). The pandemic has taught us that, in a post-Genesis 3 world, nothing can be taken for granted; gratitude, simplicity, and generosity will never go out of style, especially for those who know the God revealed in the plot of salvation.

And yet, the story told in the Bible also prevents us from tossing the pendulum to the opposite extreme, presuming that we should always wait for the worst to happen. Some Christians seem to like this idea: the world will one day be destroyed, so the best one can do is wait for its catastrophic end. In the light of our discussion, however, it is unreasonable to take such a pessimistic stance. Genesis 3 is not the final word. The plot of salvation tells us instead that the same God who created the heavens and the earth, and called the cosmos "very good," remained committed to rescuing his creation and restoring his image bearers. And precisely because he never changed his mind regarding making the universe his sacred space, he called Abraham, formed Israel, chose David, and himself reversed the problem of chaos and death in Jesus Christ.

What has the final word in our future, then, is not the chaos following Genesis 3, but the empty tomb following Jesus's crucifixion. Yes, pandemics, financial hardships, and political crises will constantly evoke the graveyard, but thanks to the Creator God, who throughout the plot of salvation remained the same, the graveyard is not forever. We can confidently join the apostle Paul in declaring, "Where, O death, is your victory? Where, O death, is your sting?" (1 Cor 15:55; cf. Hos 13:14), and make the words of the seventeenth-century poet John Donne our own:

> Death, be not proud, though some have called thee
> Mighty and dreadful, for thou art not so. . . .
> One short sleep past, we wake eternally
> And death shall be no more; Death, thou shalt die.

Death has become an inexorable fact after sin, but the resurrection of Jesus gives us the unshakable assurance that our ultimate destination is eternal life in the new creation. So, while we may agree with the saying that nothing is certain except death and taxes, the plot of salvation gives us a certainty that is firmer than any other: the cemetery has been conquered; death and the consequences of the fall no longer determine our ultimate future.

Indeed, this is what the last book of the Bible, particularly in its last two chapters, tells us with such vivid imagery. In a much more acute way than us today, the earliest readers of Revelation were going through a time of profound uncertainty. The book was written during a period in which the rules of the Roman imperial cult were hardened – probably in the last decade of the first century, under the rule of Domitian (cf. Eusebius, *Ecclesiastical History* 3 and 5) – and hence the persecution of Christians was severely intensified, as they refused to worship "the image of the beast" (Rev 13:11–15). This explains the many exhortations to perseverance that the risen Christ gives to the seven churches in Asia Minor (2:1 – 3:22).

Contrary to popular conceptions of Revelation, the book does not provide the reader with an "enigmatic map" for deciphering when exactly the "end of the world" will take place. Revelation is a portrait of Jesus's lordship over the nations and human history overall, given in a context where everything seems to be falling apart. It is the "revelation of Jesus Christ" (1:1), the one who is "the first and the last" (1:17) and possesses "the keys of Death and of Hades" (1:18), the "Lamb standing as if it had been slaughtered, having seven horns and seven eyes, which are the seven spirits of God sent out into all the earth" (5:6), the only one capable of opening "the scroll and its seven seals" (5:5), whose blood washes and whitens the garments of those who overcome evil by walking the way of the cross (7:14). The purpose of the book, therefore, is not to give easy answers to the ambiguities of everyday life, much less to suggest that the so-called "number of the beast" can be secretly implemented in the global population through vaccines (cf. 13:16–19).[1] Rather, by means of highly symbolic language, it encourages the people of God to see things, not least their ordeal under Caesar, from the heavenly perspective.[2] It is precisely for this reason that the single most repeated thing John does in Revelation is "to see" what really happens in the realm of Christ's domain – the real meaning of the historical events of his time. And the last two chapters of the book are crucial, for they depict the concluding vision of the whole plot of salvation.

So what exactly does John see at the end of Revelation that is so central for the Christian imagination about the future? If I had to sum up the vision in just one word, I would choose "consummation." The description of what awaits us in Revelation 21–22 is surprisingly binary. I say this because "binary" is everything the world after Genesis 3 is not. The present world is profoundly inconsistent and ambiguous, constantly reminding us of how good the cosmos is and at the same time how hard life in it can be. I have lost count of how many times I have gone to maternity hospitals and funerals on the same day. One moment we celebrate a blessing, the next hour we mourn a loss. But if we pay attention to the picture John offers us, we see that the experiences which have made life in the present world incomplete will finally dissipate in the world to come. It is not that we will become "flat," one-dimensional beings, but rather that we will be full and free like the risen Christ. The binary-ness of John's depiction of the world to come speaks of its perfect harmony.

Darrell Johnson perceptively comments that, at the end of the plot of salvation, everything relating to sin is absent and everything that has always been part of God's plan for the cosmos is present.[3] The future awaiting us will be thoroughly emancipated from the destructive effects of human autonomy.

---

1. Scholars agree that the number "six-hundred sixty six" is a symbolic reference to the anti-gospel imperial logic, represented by the two beasts and the image in Revelation 13. The number "six" in Revelation represents incompleteness, in contrast to seven. But the crucial detail is that the mark is said to have been placed "on the right hand or the forehead" of the inhabitants of the earth (Rev 13:16). This is an evil parody of God's Torah, as YHWH had commanded the Israelites to "bind" his words in their minds and in their actions: "Hear, O Israel: The LORD is our God, the LORD alone. You shall love the LORD your God with all your heart, and with all your soul, and with all your might. Keep these words that I am commanding you today in your heart. . . . Bind them as a sign on your hand, fix them as an emblem on your forehead" (Deut 6:4–6, 8). For further discussion, see Beale, *Book of Revelation*, 718–28.

2. This is one of the ways the genre of Jewish apocalyptic, consistently deployed in Revelation, works. Compare Revelation with Daniel 7, for example, and notice the use of extraordinary "beast" imagery and numbers so as to interpret historical events through a "heavenly" perspective – a perspective which is the very content of what is revealed. The Greek term *apokalypsis* means "revelation." For further discussion on apocalyptic as a genre, see Collins, *Apocalyptic Imagination*.

3. Johnson, *Discipleship on the Edge*, Kindle loc. 6507–743.

Since Jesus subdued sin and reversed its power, the world to come will reflect Christ's own glorious existence, not the decaying nature of the descendants of Adam and Eve. The consummation of our salvation is thus best imagined as resembling not some*thing*, but some*one*: Jesus, the one who conquered death and appointed us heirs of his life.

Accordingly, in the future awaiting us, all the dilemmas that have plagued the world since the fall will be resolved. In the post-Revelation 21 world, there will be "a new heaven and a new earth" (21:1), where the Creator will fully manifest himself among us, with no restrictions: "And I heard a loud voice from the throne saying, 'See, the home of God is among mortals. He will dwell with them; they will be his peoples, and God himself will be with them'" (21:3). Because his presence will be accessible to all, he himself will be our comfort – everything will make sense. There will be complete healing for our physical and emotional traumas, and the sins with which we still struggle today will belong to the past. We will be able once again to hold in our arms our loved ones in Christ, from whom the graveyard separated us. Happiness will be perfect, uninterrupted. We will know God and one another as God himself knows us. Jesus will be the Shepherd King of everyone, and the nations will follow his wisdom.

In the post-Revelation 21 world, there will be no more chaos – this is what the "sea" no longer existing probably connotes (21:1). Given that the divine presence will be fully accessible, we will no longer need to separate the pure from the impure. We will finally understand that the possessions and gifts which God generously bestowed on us were never ours in the first place – it was all his. We will no longer hear about social injustice, war and strife, misunderstandings, crimes, deceit, lies, immorality, betrayal, idolatry, arrogance, stray bullets, human trafficking, money embezzlement, or any other kind of violence among human beings. Read these words: "Death will be no more; mourning and crying and pain will be no more, for the first things have passed away" (21:4). This is our future, which nothing and no one can steal from us.

In short, "a new heaven and a new earth" is the culmination of the cosmos as the dwelling place of God. In the end, God will permanently move into our midst. This is why there will be no temple in the New Jerusalem, and the city itself will share attributes that hearken back to God's sacred space: the preciousness, the measurements, and the shape of the New Jerusalem (cf. 21:9–21) respectively allude to the garden of Eden, the completeness of the creation, and to the most holy place in the Old Testament (cf. Gen 2:10–14; 1 Kgs 6:14–22).

At this point, it is important to note that the certainty of this future is based on the fact that Christ is risen and the Spirit already dwells among his people (cf. Eph 1:14), not on something we do. John could have this vision only because Jesus has "the keys of Death and of Hades" (Rev 1:18). Our future is guaranteed, in other words, because the Lamb emptied the tomb in order to sit on the throne of the universe. As with the creation of the cosmos, its final restoration depends on God – and this is why we can rest assured. The consummation of the new creation is something that will come "down out of heaven from God" (21:2).

And yet, while this story is written by God alone – both as its author and as its main character – we are no mere spectators. According to John, the New Jerusalem will not represent a return to the garden of Eden. In fact, in Revelation 22:1–5, the world to come is not portrayed as a garden, but as a city with a garden in it:

> Then the angel showed me the river of the water of life, bright as crystal, flowing from the throne of God and of the Lamb through the middle of the street of the city. On either side of the river is the tree of life with its twelve kinds of fruit, producing its fruit each month; and the leaves of the tree are for the healing of the nations. Nothing accursed will be found there any more. But the throne of God and of the Lamb will be in it, and his servants will worship him; they will see his face, and his name will be on their foreheads. And there will be no more night; they need no light of lamp or sun, for the Lord God will be their light, and they will reign forever and ever.

The image of a city representing "a new heaven and a new earth" indicates that the plot of salvation includes the redemption even of that which was originally a human idealization. The reader will recall that the first major city in the Bible is Babel (cf. Gen 11:1–9), a paradigm of human arrogance. In the biblical story, the Eden project had to be interrupted due to sin, and it was human autonomy that occasioned the rise of the cities. Thanks to the restoration of the human vocation, however, the final redemption of the cosmos will contemplate a New Jerusalem, at the center of which the tree of life will be seen. Indeed, the very image of the city represents not only a place, but the very people of God, "prepared as a bride adorned for her husband" (21:2). I quote my colleague Estevan Kirschner:

> Although the city most clearly represents sin, opposition to God, and the failure of the human project, it is precisely the concept

of the perfect, ideal city that becomes the synthesis of humanity's redemption in Christ. And this is the definitive and permanent image of redemption in the last pages of the Bible.[4]

To participate in the plot of salvation, therefore, is to have our minds shaped by this future. If Jesus's resurrection has guaranteed our future, it is this future that must now guide our present. Is it not true that we would have lived differently had we known that a global pandemic was just around the corner? We may or may not admit this, but the way we live today is deeply influenced by what we believe regarding tomorrow. Hence Paul encourages his readers to persevere in continuing the work initiated by the God who raised Jesus from the dead: "But in fact Christ has been raised from the dead. . . . Therefore, my beloved, be steadfast, immovable, always excelling in the work of the Lord, because you know that in the Lord your labor is not in vain" (1 Cor 15:20, 58).

To be saved is to be liberated from despair, emptiness, fear of tomorrow. To be saved is to have hope – it is to live in hope. Admittedly, hope is the last thing I feel when I look at myself or read the newspaper. But it is precisely when we look at ourselves and read the newspaper – when our eyes are wet over our own brokenness and the sufferings of the world – that we can remember: the God of salvation, the one who never failed to fulfill his promises, "will wipe every tear from [our] eyes" (Rev 21:4). The biblical hope does not invite us to pretend everything is OK; it is the assurance that, "even though I walk through the darkest valley" (Ps 23:4), our Lord Jesus, the Good Shepherd who gave his life and took it back (John 10:11–18), emptied the tomb and sat on the throne of the universe. This hope is the certainty that the fall is not the final word. While it is true that Genesis 3 still causes us to weep, we can cry in hope because of Jesus. And now that we have walked through the plot of salvation, we can face our circumstances, knowing the end of the story. The one who never forgets to keep his promises says: "See, I am making all things new. . . . See, I am coming soon! Blessed is the one who keeps the words of the prophecy of this book" (Rev 21:5; 22:7). Jesus is risen. We will rise like him. And we will live with God in a fully restored cosmos.

---

4. Kirschner, 27 (my translation).

Conclusion

The Story Goes On

Now that we have finished our overview of the plot of salvation, we may briefly reflect on how our everyday lives should be affected by what God has accomplished in the life, death, and resurrection of Jesus Christ. The words of Samwise Gamgee concerning the great never-ending tales remind us that the biblical story goes on and invites us to find ourselves in it. How, then, are we to live it today?

There is so much to ponder in this regard. How does the gospel adjust our comprehension of the ways the church can more effectively engage in evangelism and cross-cultural mission? Given the biblical hope for a restored cosmos, what role should Christians play in addressing current environmental problems? How must we position ourselves in the face of the perennial challenges of social injustice and racism? What does it mean in practical terms to be the people of peace within societies experiencing political turmoil? Does the biblical claim that Christ is Lord over the entire universe have any implications for our ecclesiology, our public liturgies, our prayer life, our civil duties, and the way we educate our children? What about the gifts of the Holy Spirit?

We do not have enough space – and I certainly lack the expertise – to tackle all these issues. My aim in preaching the twenty sermons adapted in this book was simply to provide a clear biblical framework through which the community I serve as a pastor could interpret their lives against the ups and downs of the coronavirus pandemic. And I sincerely hope I have succeeded in convincing the reader to agree with C. S. Lewis's famous conclusion: "I believe in Christianity as I believe that the Sun has risen, not only because I see it, but because by it I see everything else."[1]

That said, I would like to say a few words by way of suggesting how to integrate our understanding of the plot of salvation with the specific – usually

---

1. Lewis, *Weight of Glory*, Kindle loc. 1267.

not so glamorous – parts each one of us plays from Monday to Sunday. Ever since we talked about Jesus's resurrection in the fifteenth chapter of this book, we have stressed the fact that, thanks to God's definitive work in Christ, the divine presence now dwells within the church. The difficulty which almost every Christian faces, however, has to do not so much with what we experience when we gather to worship, but rather with living as disciples of the risen Jesus during the rest of the week outside the sanctuary: we are surrounded by values which often contrast with – and at times oppose – the character of the God revealed in the biblical story. So as soon as Monday arrives, we are not infrequently struck by a deep sense of displacement, as though we were exiles in our own land as a result of belonging to the true Lord of the world.

At this point, we may borrow from what Miroslav Volf, Amy Sherman, Andy Crouch, and others have argued in detail,[2] and point out two temptations that we are to resist: the "permissive" stance – that is, a stance of uncritical assimilation of the culture surrounding us – and the "sectarian" stance – that is, a stance of confinement, by which we supposedly insulate ourselves from the culture surrounding us. The former assumes a fragmented view of the world and restricts the gospel merely to "private" affairs, hence encouraging a duplicity of life wherein our Mondays do not converse at all with Jesus's teaching about the kingdom of God. We sing our beautiful songs on Sundays, but end up living just like anyone else on the other six days. The latter is the flip side of the same token: the "work of God" is thought almost exclusively to concern "religious" matters, and so our involvement outside church programs must be aimed only at proselytizing the world or "winning souls for Christ." Work is seen as a "necessary evil," and serving Christ comes down to using "gospel verbiage" among unbelievers.

But none of these represents a faithful response to the plot of salvation. Christ has all authority in heaven and on earth, and therefore the whole of our lives, not least what happens on Mondays, must be shaped by his lordship. In the biblical gospel, there is no chasm separating the different "areas" of our lives – we are called to walk in the light of Jesus's resurrection in whatever activities we may be involved in. The best stance, then, is one of engagement.[3]

---

2. Volf, *Public Faith*; Sherman, *Kingdom Calling*; and Crouch, *Culture Making*. See also Stevens, *Other Six Days*; and Keller and Alsdorf, *Every Good Endeavor*; and the ten-video resource ReFrame, available at https://www.reframecourse.com.

3. Volf, *Public Faith*, 77–97.

Indeed, Paul compares his ministry to the role of an "ambassador" (2 Cor 5:20) and calls the church in Philippi "citizens of heaven" (Phil 3:20).[4] This is relevant, since an ambassador represented the emperor's interests in a distant land, and Roman citizens were expected to nurture the core values of the empire wherever they were. These terms thus offer adequate categories for us to imagine how our Christian vocation should be carried out in everyday life. And here is a key feature of an embassy: it is a microcosm of the land it represents – it stands for the very intersection of the country of origin and the territory where it is located. Furthermore, Paul preached in cities at a considerable distance from Rome – such as Philippi – which nevertheless preserved quintessentially Roman ideals (Paul and Silas were accused of subverting Roman customs in Acts 16:20–21). To be called a "citizen of heaven" is to have the focus of our lives thoroughly redefined by the kingdom of God.

When we think of the Christian calling in terms of being "ambassadors of Christ" and "citizens of heaven," the mistake which leads us to take either a "permissive" or a "sectarian" stance can be corrected. There should be no conflict of interest between our experiences at church and those outside its buildings. As ambassadors of the risen Jesus and citizens under his rule, we are to make every aspect of our existence – our homes, our professions, our relationships, our public engagements – points of intersection where kingdom values become visible and intelligible.[5] Being a disciple of Jesus therefore involves cultivating a clear vision of God's self-disclosure through the plot of salvation, which happens more tangibly at church, and making every effort to apply that vision, whether with words or deeds, to whatever task we may be entrusted with in society. Again, there are numerous observations one could make in trying to put this into practice. But let me conclude by underscoring just three key words which, in my view, help us orient our daily decisions as ambassadors of Christ and citizens of his kingdom.

The first and most important one is "character." All the practical exhortations in the New Testament, when not concerning the content of the gospel proper, reinforce the call for us to follow the example of Christ. The very story outlined in the previous pages of this book, after all, tells us about how God revealed his character. Accordingly, we are ambassadors of Christ

---

4. Cho, "Reino de Cristo," 28–38.

5. This idea was first advocated by the proponents of what came to be known as "integral mission" – most famously, René Padilla, Samuel Escobar, and Orlando Costas. For a brief overview, see Cavalcanti, *Utopia Possível*; and Kirkpatrick, "Origins of Integral Mission." In more recent years, Pedro Lucas Dulci has articulated this emphasis within the framework of the relationship between nature and grace. See Dulci, *Ortodoxia Integral*.

and citizens of his kingdom by living according to the teaching of Israel's Messiah – the one who lived a life that defeated death itself – everywhere, all the time, in whatever we do: "be imitators of God, as beloved children, and live in love, as Christ loved us" (Eph 5:1–2).

Related to this, the second key word that is worth noting is "faithfulness." The whole problem called "sin" came into being due to humanity's willingness to do things their own way. But to be a Christian is to have the way of Jesus as the supreme point of reference. So being faithful to his words in our day-to-day responsibilities is better than being "successful" (cf. Matt 7:21–27). At this point, however, many of us forget that we are called "Christians" for a reason. At times, we find ourselves in "undesired" positions and are tempted to slack, as if only the "important" things were worthy of our attention. Conversely, there are circumstances wherein we see the possibility of "success" at the expense of central ethical principles, and we are tempted to compromise. But we are not Christian *professionals*, but rather *Christians* who serve the Lord of the cosmos with our professions. We should therefore be careful not to "baptize" uncritically principles and practices simply because they "work." The book of Daniel provides us with an eloquent example that, occasionally, our commitment to what God has put into our hands may entail a night spent inside the lions' den.

And the third key word is one that we have repeated time and again throughout our journey thus far – namely, "redemption." In addition to the misconception that our work is about us and our personal realization, one familiar mistake is to think that Monday is a "necessary evil." The plot of salvation, however, tells us something very different: the human vocation has to do with keeping the cosmos as the sacred space in which the Creator could dwell, and Jesus rose from the dead so as to resume this purpose once and for all. The end of all human activity is to reflect God's redemptive plan in everything we do. Hence, Paul insists that "in the Lord your labor is not in vain" (1 Cor 15:58). This is no mere motivational cliché. Since Jesus is alive, we too will live with him, reaping the fruits of the work of his grace among us. James, for his part, calls us "a kind of first fruits of [God's] creatures" (Jas 1:18) – that is, signs of the world to come.

To be sure, Christians must use every opportunity to proclaim the resurrection as well as to support missionaries and social workers in concrete ways. One simply needs to read the Bible to realize that all this is not only necessary, but also desirable. But God is likewise interested in us regarding our daily activities as primary means of witnessing to the salvation he has accomplished in Christ. The biblical hope for the New Jerusalem indicates that the Lord wants to redeem *both* humanity *and* creation through human endeavor: medicine, law, the arts, entrepreneurship, farming, engineering, commerce, education, agriculture, home care, politics – you name it! Simply put: our work is not a utilitarian tool for us to reach religious ends, but the very instrument of the redemption of God's good creation, the results of which will be reaped when Jesus consummates his kingdom. Depending on the context, of course, our engagement could have different results – whether conservation, reform, resistance, or transformation. In any case, all we do has an eternal impact.

Character, faithfulness, redemption – the story goes on. "The God of peace will shortly crush Satan under your feet. The grace of our Lord Jesus Christ be with you" (Rom 16:20).

Bibliography

Alexander, T. Desmond, and Simon Gathercole, eds. *Heaven on Earth: The Temple in Biblical Theology*. Milton Keynes: Authentic Media, 2004.

Alter, Robert. *The Art of Biblical Narrative*. New York: Basic Books, 1981.

Barclay, John M. G. *Paul and the Power of Grace*. Grand Rapids: Eerdmans, 2020.

Bartholomew, Craig G., and Michael W. Goheen. *The Drama of Scripture: Finding Our Place in the Biblical Story*. Grand Rapids: Baker Academic, 2014.

Bauckham, Richard. *Gospel of Glory: Major Themes in Johannine Theology*. Grand Rapids: Baker Academic, 2015.

Beale, G. K. *The Book of Revelation*. NIGTNC. Grand Rapids, Eerdmans, 1999.

———. *The Temple and the Church's Mission: A Biblical Theology of the Dwelling Place of God*. Downers Grove: IVP Academic, 2004.

———. *Teologia Bíblica do Novo Testamento: A Continuidade Teológica do Antigo Testamento no Novo*. São Paulo: Vida Nova, 2011. (English: *A New Testament Biblical Theology: The Unfolding of the Old Testament in the New*. Grand Rapids: Baker Academic, 2011.)

Beale, G. K., and Mitchell Kim. *Deus Mora entre Nós: A Expansão do Éden para os Confins da Terra*. São Paulo: Loyola, 2014. (English: *God Dwells among Us: Expanding Eden to the Ends of the Earth*. Downers Grove: IVP Academic, 2014.)

Bonhoeffer, Dietrich. *Life Together*. Minneapolis: Fortress, 2015.

———. *Temptation*. London: SCM, 1963.

Bratt, James D, ed. *Abraham Kuyper: A Centennial Reader*. Grand Rapids: Eerdmans, 1998.

Brueggemann, Walter. *Genesis*. Louisville: Westminster John Knox, 2010.

———. *Theology of the Old Testament: Testimony, Dispute, Advocacy*. Minneapolis: Fortress, 2005.

Cavalcanti, Robinson. *A Utopia Possível: Em Busca de um Cristianismo Integral*. Viçosa: Ultimato, 1997.

Childs, Brevard S. *Biblical Theology of the Old and New Testaments: Theological Reflection on the Christian Bible*. Minneapolis: Fortress, 1992.

Cho, Bernardo. "Cidadãos do Reino de Cristo: A Identidade da Igreja na Cidade de Filipos." In *Missão Urbana: Servindo a Cristo na Cidade*, edited by Estevan F. Kirschner and Bernardo Cho, 28–38. São Paulo: Mundo Cristão, 2020.

———. *Royal Messianism and the Jerusalem Priesthood in the Gospel of Mark*. LNTS 607. London: T&T Clark Bloomsbury, 2019.

Collins, Jim. *Good to Great: Why Some Companies Make the Leap . . . and Others Don't*. New York: Harper Business, 2001.

Collins, John J. *The Apocalyptic Imagination: An Introduction to Jewish Apocalyptic Literature*. Grand Rapids: Eerdmans, 1998.

Crouch, Andy. *Culture Making: Recovering Our Creative Calling*. Downers Grove: IVP, 2013.

Cullmann, Oscar. *The Christology of the New Testament*. Louisville: Westminster John Knox, 1959.

Dulci, Pedro. *Ortodoxia Integral: Teoria e Prática Conectadas na Missão Cristã*. Uberlândia: Sal Editora, 2015.

Fee, Gordon D. *God's Empowering Presence: The Holy Spirit in the Letters of Paul*. Grand Rapids: Baker Academic, 2009.

Goodman, Martin. *A History of Judaism*. Princeton: Princeton University Press, 2019.

Han, Byung-Chul. *The Transparency Society*. Stanford: Stanford University Press, 2015.

Hays, Richard B. *Echoes of Scripture in the Gospels*. Waco: Baylor University Press, 2016.

———. *Echoes of Scripture in the Letters of Paul*. New Haven: Yale University Press, 1989.

Hooker, Morna D. "'Who Can This Be?' The Christology of Mark's Gospel." In *Contours of Christology in the New Testament*, edited by Richard N. Longenecker, 79–99. Grand Rapids: Eerdmans, 2005.

Imes, Carmen Joy. *Bearing God's Name: Why Sinai Still Matters*. Downers Grove: IVP Academic, 2019.

Johnson, Darrell. *Discipleship on the Edge: An Expository Journey through the Book of Revelation*. Vancouver: Regent College Publishing, 2004.

Jozino, Josmar. *Cobras e Lagartos: A Verdadeira História do PCC*. São Paulo: Via Leitura, 2017.

Juel, Donald. *Messianic Exegesis: Christological Interpretation of the Old Testament in Early Christianity*. Minneapolis: Fortress, 1988.

Keener, Craig S. *The Spirit in the Gospels and Acts: Divine Purity and Power*. Grand Rapids: Baker Academic, 2010.

Keller, Timothy. "Justice in the Bible," *Life in the Gospel*, Fall 2020. https://quarterly. gospelinlife.com/justice-in-the-bible/.

Keller, Timothy, and Katherine Leary Alsdorf. *Every Good Endeavor: Connecting Your Work to God's Work*. London: Penguin, 2014.

Kingsbury, Jack Dean. *Matthew as Story*. Minneapolis: Fortress, 1988.

Kirkpatrick, David C. "C. René Padilla and the Origins of Integral Mission in Post-War Latin America." *JEH* 67 (2016): 351–71.

Kirschner, Estevan F. "Da Babilônia à Nova Jerusalém: O Ensino da Bíblia sobre a Cidade." In *Missão Urbana: Servindo a Cristo na Cidade*, edited by Estevan F. Kirschner and Bernardo Cho, 17–27. São Paulo: Mundo Cristão, 2020.

Lewis, C. S. *Cristianismo Puro e Simples*. São Paulo: Martins Fontes, 2005. (English: *Mere Christianity*. San Francisco: Harper Collins, 2009.)

———. *The Great Divorce*. San Francisco: Harper One, 2015.

———. *The Weight of Glory and Other Essays*. San Francisco: Harper One, 2013.

Lincoln, Andrew T. *Ephesians*. WBC 42. Grand Rapids: Zondervan, 1990.

Longman III, Tremper. *How to Read Genesis*. Downers Grove: IVP Academic, 2005.

MacIntyre, Alasdair. *After Virtue: A Study in Moral Theory*. Notre Dame: University of Notre Dame Press, 2007.

Milgrom, Jacob. *Leviticus: A Book of Ritual and Ethics*. Minneapolis: Augsburg Fortress, 2004.

Moo, Douglas J. *The Epistle to the Romans*. NICNT. Grand Rapids: Eerdmans, 1996.

Newbigin, Lesslie. *The Gospel in a Pluralist Society*. Grand Rapids: Eerdmans, 1989.

Provan, Iain. "On Rightly Hitching Our Wagons: A Response to Andy Stanley." *Voices*, 18 May 2018. https://www.christianpost.com/voice/on-rightly-hitching-our-wagons-a-response-to-andy-stanley.html.

———. *Seriously Dangerous Religion: What the Old Testament Really Says and Why It Matters*. Waco: Baylor University Press, 2014.

Provan, Iain, V. Phillips Long, and Tremper Longman III. *A Biblical History of Israel*. Louisville: Westminster John Knox, 2003.

Rose, Martin. "Names of God in the OT." In *The Anchor Yale Bible Dictionary*, Vol. 4, edited by David Noel Freedman et al., 1001–11. New York: Doubleday, 1992.

Sandel, Michael J. *Justice: What's the Right Thing to Do?* New York: Farrar, Straus, and Giroux, 2009.

Sanders, E. P. *Jesus and Judaism*. London: SCM, 1985.

Sherman, Amy. *Kingdom Calling: Vocational Stewardship for the Common Good*. Downers Grove: IVP, 2011.

Stark, Rodney. *The Rise of Christianity: How the Obscure, Marginal Jesus Movement Became the Dominant Religious Force in the Western World in a Few Centuries*. San Francisco: Harper One, 1996.

Stevens, Paul. *The Other Six Days: Vocation, Work, and Ministry in Biblical Perspective*. Grand Rapids: Eerdmans, 2000.

Taylor, Charles. *The Ethics of Authenticity*. Cambridge: Harvard University Press, 1991.

Thiessen, Matthew. *Jesus and the Forces of Death: The Gospels' Portrayal of Ritual Impurity within First-Century Judaism*. Grand Rapids: Baker Academic, 2020.

Tolkien, J. R. R. "On Fairy Stories." In *The Monsters and the Critics, and Other Essays*, edited by Christopher Tolkien, 109–61. London: Harper Collins, 2006.

———. *The Lord of the Rings*. New York: HarperCollins, 2005.

Volf, Miroslav. *A Public Faith: How Followers of Christ Should Serve the Common Good*. Grand Rapids: Brazos, 2011.

Von Rad, Gerhard. *Old Testament Theology*. Edinburgh: Oliver & Boyd, 1962–1965.

Walton, John H. *Ancient Near Eastern Thought and the Old Testament*. Grand Rapids: Baker Academic, 2006.

———. *The Lost World of Adam and Eve: Genesis 2–3 and the Human Origins*. Downers Grove: IVP Academic, 2015.

Walton, John H., Victor H. Matthews, and Mark W. Chavalas. *The IVP Bible Background Commentary: Old Testament*. Downers Grove: IVP, 1997.

Watson, Francis. *The Fourfold Gospel: A Theological Reading of the New Testament Portraits of Jesus*. Grand Rapids: Baker Academic, 2016.

Watts, Rikk E. *Isaiah's New Exodus in Mark*. WUNT 2/88. Tübingen: Mohr Siebeck, 1997.

———. "It's about Life: A Biblical Journey." Course, Regent College, 2011.

Williams, Paul. "The Reframing Story." *Reframe Course*. Regent College, 2012.

Wright, Christopher J. H. *The Mission of God: Unlocking the Bible's Grand Narrative*. Downers Grove: IVP Academic, 2006.

———. *Old Testament Ethics for the People of God*. Downers Grove: IVP Academic, 2004.

———. *The Old Testament in Seven Sentences: A Small Introduction to a Vast Topic*. Downers Grove: IVP Academic, 2019.

Wright, N. T. *Jesus and the Victory of God*. Minneapolis: Fortress, 1996.

———. *The New Testament and the People of God*. Minneapolis: Fortress, 1992.

———. *Paul and the Faithfulness of God*. Minneapolis: Fortress, 2013.

———. *Simply Jesus: Who He Was, What He Did, Why It Matters*. London: SPCK, 2011.

Yarbro Collins, Adela. "Mark and His Readers: The Son of God among Jews." *HTR* 92 (1999): 393–408.

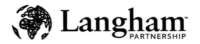 Langham
PARTNERSHIP

Langham Literature and its imprints are a ministry of Langham Partnership.

Langham Partnership is a global fellowship working in pursuit of the vision God entrusted to its founder John Stott –

> *to facilitate the growth of the church in maturity and Christ-likeness through raising the standards of biblical preaching and teaching.*

Our vision is to see churches in the Majority World equipped for mission and growing to maturity in Christ through the ministry of pastors and leaders who believe, teach and live by the word of God.

Our mission is to strengthen the ministry of the word of God through:
- nurturing national movements for biblical preaching
- fostering the creation and distribution of evangelical literature
- enhancing evangelical theological education

especially in countries where churches are under-resourced.

Our ministry

Langham Preaching partners with national leaders to nurture indigenous biblical preaching movements for pastors and lay preachers all around the world. With the support of a team of trainers from many countries, a multi-level programme of seminars provides practical training, and is followed by a programme for training local facilitators. Local preachers' groups and national and regional networks ensure continuity and ongoing development, seeking to build vigorous movements committed to Bible exposition.

Langham Literature provides Majority World preachers, scholars and seminary libraries with evangelical books and electronic resources through publishing and distribution, grants and discounts. The programme also fosters the creation of indigenous evangelical books in many languages, through writer's grants, strengthening local evangelical publishing houses, and investment in major regional literature projects, such as one volume Bible commentaries like *The Africa Bible Commentary* and *The South Asia Bible Commentary*.

Langham Scholars provides financial support for evangelical doctoral students from the Majority World so that, when they return home, they may train pastors and other Christian leaders with sound, biblical and theological teaching. This programme equips those who equip others. Langham Scholars also works in partnership with Majority World seminaries in strengthening evangelical theological education. A growing number of Langham Scholars study in high quality doctoral programmes in the Majority World itself. As well as teaching the next generation of pastors, graduated Langham Scholars exercise significant influence through their writing and leadership.

To learn more about Langham Partnership and the work we do visit **langham.org**

Lightning Source UK Ltd.
Milton Keynes UK
UKHW020931021022
409753UK00007B/83